THE KARATE WAY

Also by Dave Lowry

Autumn Lightning: The Education of an American Samurai

*In the Dojo: A Guide to the Rituals and Etiquette
of the Japanese Martial Arts*

Sword and Brush: The Spirit of the Martial Arts

THE
KARATE
WAY

Discovering the Spirit of Practice

Dave Lowry

SHAMBHALA
Boston & London
2009

Shambhala Publications, Inc.
Horticultural Hall
300 Massachusetts Avenue
Boston, Massachusetts 02115
www.shambhala.com

9 8 7 6 5 4 3 2 1

First Edition
Printed in Canada

♾ This edition is printed on acid-free paper that meets the
American National Standards Institute Z39.48 Standard.
Distributed in the United States by Random House, Inc.,
and in Canada by Random House of Canada Ltd
♻ This book was printed on 100% postconsumer recycled paper.
For more information please visit us at www.shambhala.com.

Library of Congress Cataloging-in-Publication Data
Lowry, Dave.
The Karate way: discovering the spirit of practice /
Dave Lowry.—1st ed.
p.   cm.
ISBN 978-1-59030-647-5 (pbk.: alk. paper)
1. Karate. I. Title.
GV1114.3.L694 2009
796.815'3—dc22
2008032449

For Cyna, Mina, Laura, and Matt—karateka, friends

Out of a misty dream
Our path emerges for a while, then closes
Within a dream.

—Ernest Dowson

CONTENTS

Introduction

I forewarn—and apologize. Before you are through with this book, assuming you finish it at all, you may well become irritated with my frequent use of the word "serious," as in "the serious *karateka*" or "the serious dojo." There is a whiff of the self-congratulatory smugness in this locution: "If you are serious about your *karate-do* you will perforce agree with my points and observations and if you take exception to them—well, you are not quite so serious as you ought to be." That may be the aroma you detect coming off these pages. It is not the recipe I have written here, however.

Karate-do, along with the other modern martial Ways of Japan—judo, kendo, and aikido—is at an interesting and important step of maturation in the West. There are karate practitioners here who are as accomplished, polished, and masterful as anyone practicing karate in Japan. (The same may be said of *budoka* in the other arts.) There are a great many more who have the potential to be at that level but who are, for various reasons, not there—and not headed in the right direction exactly to get there. In some instances, this will be because they are insufficiently motivated.

There is nothing necessarily wrong with that. The fellow goes to the dojo three times a week, practices hard, and does what he is told by his teacher. He has been reminded that constant repetition is the key to the eventual mastery of karate. So he makes a thousand reverse punches when that is the exercise demanded in class that night, repeats his kata one hundred times a week. He thinks at times he is improving; at other times, he feels he is stuck in the proverbial rut. It does not particularly matter. He knows perfection is an ever-receding goal—there's something Zen about it. Or so he's been told. Don't worry. Just keep at it. And truth be told, that does not bother him. He likes his dojomates. He likes the socialization of the dojo, likes the exercise; he enjoys a bit of competition now and then. He appreciates the mental challenges and benefits, emotional and psychological, from karate-do. There is something that feels good about karate and he does not feel any pressing need to question or to go any further into things. That fellow is getting what he wants from his karate. To think of it another way, he is like a mountain climber who has reached a certain elevation and is happy there. He may understand there are higher peaks in the range. Yet he will decide that, for him, this is high enough, thank you. He likes the scenery here, so he is content to knock about at that level, wandering around the mountain, exploring a little here and there at that height, yet never venturing higher.

Another karateka may be a member at that same dojo. He attends just as regularly, trains just as hard, and follows the advice and instructions of his sensei. He, too, recognizes he will never actually perfect his art, that the goals become more and more distant the harder and longer one trains. Nevertheless, he suspects there is more out there for him. There is something in the Way of karate he is not yet getting. There are pathways on the journey for which he has no map. He is like a climber who has reached a particular elevation and instead of looking around and being satisfied with his surroundings, gazes upward and wonders, "What's it like up there and how can I get there?"

From my perspective, the first karateka is sincere and honest about his art. He is simply not as *serious* as the second. It is not fair to chastise the climber who has scaled a peak to a respectable elevation and who is content with his accomplishment. I am in awe of climbers who make it to the base camp of Everest, even if they never go a step higher. Still, while not judging either and acknowledging both as mountaineers, we must make a distinction between the climber happy at base camp and the climber who pulls on his crampons and takes up his ice ax and keeps pushing higher.

Too many karateka—and budoka in general—are hiking about determinedly, going around and *around* the mountain, either believing they are actually going *higher* on it or frustrated because they sense the higher elevations and lack a route up. Too many karate sensei, well-meaning perhaps, are invested in teaching their students that they, as teachers, know the way up—"Just follow along and I will take you there"—when in truth they have climbed no higher themselves and haven't a clue how to do so.

I have not been to the top of the mountain of karate-do. I may, in fact, be only a couple steps ahead of you. I have been blessed and fortunate to have had teachers who have climbed higher and who have been generous in showing me the path. I am still following their lead. I am not yet content at the elevation where I am now. In pushing on to higher peaks, I in no way disparage those who do not want to follow or go along with me. I want more, though. I have benefited enormously by having climbed to where I am now, by taking the advice of those who have gone before. I am confident they have shown me a route that will take me to where I want to go. That may not, in the end, be to the top of the mountain. (Here the analogy breaks down; there is no final summit and it is better to think of karate not as a single peak but, as I noted before, a wonderful and extraordinary range of mountains.) But I will climb at least to the heights that I am physically, emotionally, and mentally able to scale. It is some of that advice I am presenting here.

The tone in these pages is often that of the scold, the "every-thing-you-know-is-wrong" pedant. One does not wish to be thought of in such a way, naturally. And one risks offending the reader by so often pointing out this or that inaccuracy or miscon-ception concerning karate-do and its practice. It may seem that, as much as I am pointing a way farther up the mountain, I am also criticizing the efforts of those struggling on the lower pitches of the climb. If that is so, my plea is that many karateka have been given bad information about the best way to approach the moun-tain. They have entered it on a slope that leads to nowhere and merely trails off to a dead end or that is actually dangerous and counterproductive. It does little good to instruct these karateka on going higher. They must consider the possibility that they need to go back down to the base and start out on a better, more productive route.

The nature of karate-do and all Japanese *budo* have been misrepresented in the West (and not insignificantly in the East as well)—sometimes deliberately, and sometimes with the best of intentions. The antidote to this misrepresentation is harsh. There is no easy way to explain that the path you are on is not the one you think it is and you must turn around and go back and begin again.

Please consider the case of a martial artist of my acquaintance, a man who lived for more than two decades in Japan and trained in a classical combat art there. He is thoroughly conversant in Japanese culture and language; he eventually was given latitude in teaching authority that, in a conservative art such as his, is quite rare. After going back to his home country, teaching, and gaining several students, he returned to Japan and, almost by accident, he came to the dojo of another teacher of the same art who is senior to him. The sensei looked at the man's technique as he performed some of the most difficult and advanced parts of the art's curricu-lum. The man was hoping for some fine-tuning, some polishing of detail. Instead, the sensei looked him squarely in the eye and said, "You don't know how to hold a sword."

This is a watershed moment in the life of anyone devoted to something like a martial art, someone who has spent painstaking effort and decades in training and teaching. The ego goes into full-power drive. And it is not just the ego; there is a natural skepticism: "Look, I didn't just stumble into a dojo last month. I've been at this a *long* time. I have credentials, a license to teach. I am highly respected in the community of martial arts practitioners who are expert in these old systems. You don't reach that level without some skill if you are a complete idiot or entirely incompetent."

My acquaintance was at a crucial moment. It was a moment where you laugh in the face of the sensei, confident he is wrong, and go on about your business, or you nod politely, say "thank you," and make a graceful exit before going on about your business. Or you take a third choice. It is this third choice that is initially most painful. It is the choice that, as an experienced climber, you suspect may be difficult and challenging but which, in this case at least, is the right one to take. You take a breath and say, "OK, show me how to hold it."

The man did just that. He has not regretted the decision.

I do not in any way mean to suggest I am in the position of that senior sensei or that those holding this book in their hands are in the position of the fellow who was told he did not fully understand even the rudiments of his art. I already noted that I may be only a step or two ahead of you on this climb. My thought, though, is that when we begin to believe we understand something completely, that we have a grasp on it, then we may take much of what we know for granted and extrapolate from that knowledge, and consequently we can get into trouble. Sometimes it is good to reassess, to step back and take a fresh look. My hope is that this book might be a way to help do that. Perhaps it will make you realize you do not need to go all the way back to the bottom of the mountain again; maybe you just need to consider altering your route a bit. Maybe you are on the correct route already but you need some information to get you higher.

Karate-do is a very big mountain range. One may spend a lifetime perfectly and legitimately content to circle around and around its many peaks at a certain level, satisfied and fulfilled. There are others, however, who want to go higher. Again, I cannot take them there. And obviously no book can, either. What a book might do is show them some routes they may wish to explore that might help them climb higher. It is for those karateka that this book is intended.

1

Traditional Karate

Beware any time you hear talk or read of "traditional" karate.

There are a lot of words in our daily life that have connotations, of course, beyond their dictionary meaning. Some of them can be loaded in the sense they are meant to persuade or influence us in some way. Conflating a word with a specific idea is sometimes disingenuous, and sometimes misleading. So it is with "traditional." "I am for a traditional American way of life," a politician might tell us. But what does that really mean? Sure, it can mean living civilly with our neighbors, working hard at honest labor, raising children with a sense of respect and obligation. Those have a long tradition on the American scene. But at one time or another, a "traditional" American way of life meant large numbers of children working in sweatshops. The fellow advocating a "return to traditional America" is, we can be fairly sure, not talking about the tradition in America of streets so bespotted with horse manure the air itself in many cities posed a serious health hazard to anyone walking down its avenues.

What we like to do in the case of words like "tradition" is to pick and choose what we mean when we use them. An editor once assumed I would admire a B-movie action star because in his karate training he wore a white uniform and so, at least in the imagination of the editor, he did "traditional karate." White uniforms and bowing, calling the teacher "sensei," doing lots of kata: these may be a big part of the definition, in the minds of some, of traditional karate. Serious students of the art, though, should do some long and serious thinking about what they mean when or if they use that as a way to describe what they do.

What is traditional karate? Well, it began on Okinawa, so if there is any place we might find the roots of a tradition, it would be there. In the past decade or so some extensive historical investigations into the fighting arts of Okinawa have been done. They seem to indicate that grappling methods, called *tegumi* in some places in the island chain and *mutou* in others, were popular indigenous methods of combat. This is not surprising. The human body takes more easily and naturally to wrestling, to the grabbing and entangling of limbs, than it does to striking. It is impossible to know for sure, but it is a good guess that systems of combat featuring strikes were either introduced from Chinese sources or those sources were a powerful influence on any striking arts that might have been practiced on Okinawa. Books on karate history usually acknowledge this. It is important to understand, however, that the punching and kicking systems of fighting brought by the Chinese (or by native Okinawans who had visited China) did not instantly replace grappling, nor did they develop on Okinawa separately. Instead, they appear to have been integrated into the native forms of wrestling there. Okinawan karate traditionally included a lot of grappling. Older forms of the art still taught there and elsewhere continue with this emphasis. Striking methods are combined with grappling, with the assumption that an encounter will involve both. Even in those Okinawan karate systems that evolved extensively after they were brought to mainland Japan and that place a much greater focus on striking, one can still see the remnants of this grappling-striking symbiosis. Open hand techniques in a karate kata usually indicate, for example, that the motion was originally a grab, or some technique designed to take hold of an opponent, either for a joint lock or throw. The older the kata, in fact, the more open hand movements it tends to have— a feature we can see in kata like Rohai and the early versions of Patsai or Passai, called Bassai in their Japanese forms.

Those who teach what they imagine to be traditional karate might be surprised at the way their predecessors took on the teaching role on Okinawa during the eighteenth and nineteenth centuries, when historical accounts of the art first became extensive enough for us to gather some reliable glimpses of it. Today, the karate sensei is usually in constant motion, demonstrating for the class or walking through it as the members practice, making corrections and giving further instruction. He or she counts the cadence for sequences of kata or basic movements. This was not the standard way an Okinawan karate teacher taught. Probably influenced by Chinese modes of giving instruction, the teacher sat quite still and watched. He might sit on a raised platform, like the verandas that surrounded some Okinawan homes, or on the ground. Students of some of the renowned karate masters of the late nineteenth and early twentieth centuries recall entire training sessions in which their teachers never moved, and only made some verbal corrections, if that. At other times, the teacher would rise to demonstrate a technique then return to his seat while his students put the example into practice. One of my karate sensei had been taught this way.

"Teachers used to believe if they were walking around, moving, they would miss details," he told me. "They would demonstrate a technique or some part of the kata they wanted us to do, then they would sit and watch and never move a muscle." He described these lessons as "intimidating." That may sound odd. It sounds, indeed, as if the teacher is not really involved in the class. "But those eyes," my sensei remembered, "you could feel them boring into you." When the teacher is walking through the class, there will be those moments when a student will know

the attention won't be on him. Students quickly develop a sense
of when the teacher's attention is directed elsewhere. Consciously or unconsciously, the students slack off or pick up the
pace accordingly. With the teacher sitting and watching the entire
class, it is impossible to detect if he or she is paying, at any one
moment, specific attention to you. Consequently, you feel under
the teacher's gaze incessantly. Further, lacking any kind of body
language from the teacher that could indicate approval or dis-
gust, the karateka who trained under a largely motionless teacher
was clueless. Was his technique good or bad? "You had to learn
to trust yourself," my sensei explained, "to believe you were doing
it right and to conduct yourself that way, even if you weren't getting any reinforcement from the teacher."

If you have an image of traditional nineteenth-century karate
practitioners performing their kata in starched white *keikogi,*
you need to revise it. Karate was practiced either in the normal
clothes worn by Okinawans in their daily life or in loincloths or
short pants. Doubtless one reason for the light clothing in karate
training on Okinawa was the weather. Okinawa is tropical; the
heat and humidity there can be oppressive. So training in simple,
light clothing was practical. Moreover, practicing karate bare-
chested was considered "scientific" by some Okinawan karate
teachers. Accounts of the era, of karate practice done in this manner, frequently refer to it in admiring terms. Why? One possible
answer is that as Okinawan karate became more sophisticated
by continuing relationships with Chinese combat arts experts,
Okinawans began concentrating on some of the finer details,
especially of the Chinese internal arts like tai chi. These arts
stress subtle muscle movements and stretching of tendons and
ligaments, which cannot be seen when one is wearing clothing.
Nakedness, at least from the waist up, allowed the teacher to assess the movement. Anything that reflected a Chinese influence
would have been highly regarded and recognized as advanced.
It is ironic: today, looking at photos of karateka from those days,
bare save for a loincloth, one may think of the karate at that time

as primitive. In fact, those posing for the photos would likely have thought just the opposite.

The idea of a dojo, if we are talking about "traditional karate" in the sense of the Okinawan original, will also have to be discarded. Almost all karate training took place outside, on natural terrain. Instruction was given around the home of the teacher or in areas sufficiently private to be away from observers who might steal the secrets. Okinawan karateka sometimes used the term *miya* to describe outdoor places where the art was transmitted. It is a word borrowed from Japanese Shinto, referring to a shrine. "That's not what our ancestors called it, though," an older Okinawan karate practitioner told me. "That is a modern borrowed word from the Japanese." He explained that training sites for karate were called in Uchinanchu, the native language of the islands, *ugan* or *utaki*. The former is a public shrine or sacred spot. The latter means "a tall peak." Both words have religious and spiritual connotations in native Okinawan folk practices as well as in the political history of the island chain. Ugan were groves set aside for certain ceremonies while utaki were the sites of fortresses ("fortified estates" might be a better translation) where, prior to the fourteenth century, political and social power was centered on Okinawa. Teaching and practicing karate in such special places would have added an air of the sacred or extraordinary to it. And locating the training site in such an area, away from normal activities, would have added another barrier of privacy.

Aside from a lack of documentation about its early development, the most significant problem in defining "traditional" karate is teasing the original threads of Okinawan karate from the tapestry of Japanese budo (and Japanese culture in general) into which it was eventually so deeply interwoven. Once karate was brought to mainland Japan in the early twentieth century, it was gradually incorporated into the existing combat arts there, in terms of the spirit and manner in which it was propagated. The expatriate Okinawan teachers often did this weaving themselves. Eager to have their art accepted, they adopted Japanese martial concepts, teaching methods, grading systems, and organization. So many of the so-called traditional aspects we associate with karate—the black belt, the hierarchical structure of karate associations and organizations, the progressive and graduated curriculum—are not in any way Okinawan (and thus not "traditional") but rather are from mainland Japan. Ideas we think of as thoroughly fundamental to karate are also often not indigenous to karate as it was traditionally practiced and transmitted on Okinawa. The *ikken hisastu,* or "killing with a single blow," for instance, is not a salient aspect of Okinawan karate. It is a concept derived entirely from Japanese swordsmanship, where the possibility of taking life with one sword strike was a combat reality. Early karate pioneers in Japan adopted this concept and integrated it into their teaching because it made their art seem more Japanese and therefore more palatable to Japanese students. Again, there is a distinct irony: Japanese karateka who traveled to China after Japan invaded and occupied that country, and who saw Chinese arts for the first time, often commented that instead of concentrating power in what was meant to be a single, devastating blow, as the Japanese did in their "Japanese karate," the Chinese approach was to make a series of barrage-like strikes to overcome any defense. What they did not know was that this latter style of fighting was far more traditional in karate than the "one strike kill" mentality in which they had trained. The Japanese were, in a sense, seeing "traditional karate" for the first time.

So, how do we define "tradition" in our karate-do? And why is it something important for us to define, something to think about? At least we can agree it is more than wearing a white keikogi.

2

Keeping It in Gear

Some years ago, while writing for a financial magazine, I interviewed the author of a best-selling book on stretching and conditioning. In addition to his book, the author regularly gave seminars to teach people to get into shape or to stay that way. He told me something I found fascinating, about speaking to a group of railroad workers who were in real need of better physical fitness. Virtually every one of these guys, he told me, was in terrible shape: overweight, about as flexible as a doorknob. Their work on the railroad was physically demanding. They were active all day long. But once they got home, they told him, the remainder of their waking hours consisted of nothing more strenuous than plopping in front of the TV, demolishing a bag or two of potato chips, and drinking a couple of six-packs.

To be sure, sloth and physical inactivity and the resultant problems—obesity, high blood pressure, and so on—are all too common in the modern world. What was unusual about this group, the author told me, was that such habits were not lifelong by any means. To the contrary, he discovered that nearly all of the railroad workers had in their younger years been active high school athletes. The majority had played at the varsity level in football or basketball and many had in fact been on championship teams. These were guys who, less than twenty years earlier, had been in the top 5 percent or so of the population in terms of their conditioning and fitness. And now, still in their mid-thirties, they were slugs. What happened?

The author explained that during their high school years, physical training and workouts for their sports had consumed a considerable portion of their days, but when they had graduated and joined the workforce, exercise outside of the physical efforts required for their occupations virtually disappeared from their lives. "There was nothing in between for them," he told me. "Their engines were either in overdrive like they were in high school, or they were idling like they were when I met them."

Unfortunately, this approach to fitness is common in our society. Physical activity—playing games or being active—is still seen by a lot of people as a pursuit for children. "I ran into an old high school buddy who'd started karate practice when I did," a friend told me recently. "When he found I was still practicing thirty years later, he said 'I can't believe you're still into that foolishness. You're too old for that!'" This attitude is seen, in some variation, in budo training. I am not talking about the "too old for that" mindset, but rather the attitude that too many budoka have, that if they cannot practice at full speed, they are not going to practice at all.

This attitude is predominant in Japanese karate-do. I think I know why. Some background about the Japanese system of education is necessary to explain it. In Japan, high school is a massive, daunting grind. Long, long hours are spent studying. There is little time for anything else in the life of most students. After attending classes all day, many students are off to private academies in the afternoon that prepare them for college exams, then they return home to hours of homework. But if your grades and tests are high enough in high school, you make it into a good university. And at that point, you can coast, educationally speaking. College in Japan is popularly seen as a time for slacking off, for having fun before adulthood begins. While there are exceptions, undergraduate college and university courses are relatively easy by the standards of many other countries. Study outside class in most Japanese colleges and universities does not take anywhere near the time Japanese high school students spend at it. Instead, college students in Japan devote a lot more time to various club activities than they do in study. Universities and colleges have numerous clubs and social organizations.

Karate clubs are popular in a lot of Japanese universities. They have been since before the Second World War, largely as a result of the efforts of Gichin Funakoshi. Funakoshi was determined to elevate the status of karate. In the years after he and other Okinawan practitioners introduced it to Japan, karate had a reputation as a thug's style of fighting. Actually, before that, it was thought of as a sort of country bumpkin's form of fisticuffs, the sort of common brawling that might be acceptable for the lower classes but which would, of course, never be of much interest to the sophisticated Japanese. Unlike the aristocratic roots of judo or kendo, karate had no samurai lineage. It was the product of Okinawans, who were considered rubes and hillbillies by the average Japanese at that time. Karate had an unsavory reputation, something engaged in by ruffians and organized crime enforcers such as the *yakuza*. The so-called karate wars of the 1930s in Kyoto and Nara—beatings and vandalism inflamed by communists and labor strife in Japan—did much to reinforce this violent, thuggish image. To combat it, Funakoshi and others went to lengths to get karate instituted as a club activity in universities. They were significantly successful in their efforts. Virtually all the famous karate teachers who came to the United States in the 1960s were graduates of places like Takushoku and other schools that had strong karate clubs.

It is not unusual for university karate club members to train five or six hours a day. Their dedication is on a whole different level than that found in the typical karate dojo. It is a "gung ho, rah-rah, let's punch the *makiwara* until our knuckles fall off" approach that can, if it doesn't kill or cripple them, turn young college-age men and women into phenomenally good karateka. And, not co-incidentally, as I just noted, who is it who introduced karate to the rest of the world back in the late 1950s and early 1960s? With some exceptions, it was recent graduates of Japanese universities. They came to the United States and to Europe, fresh from having trained almost as much as they slept, and they brought that attitude toward karate with them. In other instances, karate was brought back from Japan by U.S. military personnel who had experienced a similar training environment. Outside of their daily military duties, many of them had lots of free time to spend in training. So they, too, introduced a mentality of karate (or other budo) practice as a seven-days-a-week type of activity, one that required a certain near-fanaticism for inculcating the "proper" spirit.

There is nothing inherently wrong with this kind of devotion. It can lead, however, to an unbalanced view of karate-do. Look: outside of these university students, rabidly enthusiastic foreigners coming to Japan to train, or attendees at special practice sessions, almost nobody in Japan does a modern budo every day of the week. For most Japanese, the train ride to the dojo alone is too much, requiring an hour or more of the day. Even if a work schedule would permit it, daily attendance at a dojo is not something in which the average adult Japanese budoka engages. Instead, once they are out of school and working full time, they have to cut back in their training. Sometimes, like the railroad workers, they will make the same mistake. "If I can't do it at an intense, nearly full-time level, I'm not gonna do it at all" is their attitude. This mentality is just as misguided there among budoka as it is among former high school or college athletes here.

The truth is, age, family and personal responsibilities, and a career all make demands on adults. Frankly, I would be a little suspicious of an adult who is in the dojo every night of the week.

Karate-do and other budo are supposed to enhance our lives, not become a substitute for the realities of life. That we move on as we grow up, tackling careers and building relationships, does not mean we have to give up our training. We must, however, learn to go from overdrive—if we have been training that hard—to a more relaxed gear that will take us into middle age and beyond, still active in our art.

Sadly, too many karate teachers try to perpetuate these artificial expectations of training. I have heard of teachers who tell their students that skipping even a single class will reduce their reaction time by this or that percentage, or some other such silliness. Perhaps these reductions in performance—probably measurable only under laboratory conditions—may have some possible effect if one is competing at an international level. Whether the forty-five-year-old *nidan* will note a significant dip in his progress because he wasn't able to train at last Thursday's class is something else again. And one suspects these dire warnings have less to do with a demand for peak performance among the students than they do with a possible slacking off in their attendance, which might result in a concomitant reduction in dojo income.

It is unrealistic to believe karate-do or other budo will have no value in your life if you cannot devote several hours every day to it as you may have when you were single, childless, unemployed, or otherwise free to train long hours. Of course, it is equally absurd to think you are going to get anywhere by giving only an hour a week to your practice or that you can regularly skip classes. Budo is not like a bridge club, where you drop in when you have nothing better to do. It is an art that will always make greater demands on your time than would most hobbies or avocations. Still, this must be put in perspective. Learn to maximize the time you *do* spend in the dojo. Understand that the time we have for budo is not a fixed amount and that at periods of life, we may have to cut back, and that this does not mean we are no longer going to benefit from our art. Just because you cannot be in the dojo every night of the week, like you were back when you were in college or employed only part-time, does not mean it is time to quit altogether, that your training is no longer worth it. Just because you may not, at the age of thirty-five, do what you could at nineteen, does not mean there is no longer any reason to continue with your karate. There is a reason cars and bicycles have more than one gear. If you ignore the potential of training in gears other than maximum overdrive, you may never realize the rewards that taking it slower can provide.

3

What Do You Think about a Good Bad Teacher?

The opportunity to interview karateka, either students or teachers, does not arise very often for me. That's good, because when it does I usually pass. I am not skilled as an interviewer—which is a gracious way to try to say that from my experience most karateka do not have much of anything original or provocative or intriguing to say. There are certainly exceptions. I have met some extraordinary people who also happen to be karateka. (Funny how that works: karate tends to be one facet—an important one but still, only one—in these unusual people. Yet when karate is all I have in common with them or all that makes them different, I find them not all that interesting.) When I meet one of those exceptions, interviewing him or her or just talking, I try to slip in my favorite question. It is one that fascinates me. Invariably, I find the answers to be informative. The question: Suppose there was a karate teacher whose skills you admire and who is, in a technical sense, an excellent instructor. He or she is also, as a human being,

a total jerk. Spouse abuser. Philanderer. Drunk. Someone you
wouldn't invite into your home in a thousand years but someone who has karate abilities that you wish to have too. Someone
who can teach them to you. Would you apprentice yourself to
such a person?

Perhaps another way of putting it would be this: how important is a potential sensei's character? Is it more or equally as important as talents and ability to transmit those talents? However
you put it, this can be a tough question. Good (and by "good" here
I mean good purely in a technical sense) teachers of karate are to
be had, though they are not exactly falling out of trees around us.
I live in a major urban area, one where a check through the phone
book reveals three full pages of martial arts instruction, including
dozens of karate training centers. I do not know the people teaching there. And perhaps I am jaded. But put it this way: if I had to
judge from their ads alone, I don't think there are any I would
really consider having as a real teacher. A really good teacher, let's
face it, is hard to find. This is true everywhere, even in Japan. So
let's say you have always wanted to study karate-do. And right
down the street from you opens a karate dojo, run by a teacher of
high rank, one with a reputation as a technical instructor that is
unsurpassed. You are ready to sign up the next day. Before you do,
though, you call a few karateka friends elsewhere in the country
who know this teacher. The conversations reveal some sordid details. The teacher regularly makes sexual advances, crude and obvious, to young women when he is out in other places and giving
seminars. He occasionally indulges in illicit drugs. There is nothing that interferes with his teaching substantially. His ability to
teach you to punch is unalloyed by his personal behavior, you are
assured by those who know him. They reveal his awful conduct
but insist they have learned much about the art of karate from
him. That aside, his behavior outside the dojo is unacceptable,
at least to you. What would you do in this instance? Go study
with him, assuming that your own moral character will grant you
immunity from the more pernicious aspects of your teacher's

personality, allowing you only to absorb what is technically good? Or pass on the opportunity, hoping that by some stroke of luck another, similarly qualified karate teacher might just happen to drop out of the sky tomorrow and open a dojo on the other side of the street, a teacher who is as well a moral person? Sure, most of us would, all things being equal, prefer to become the student of a good teacher who is also a good person. What about, though, when he is the latter, but not the former?

The simple argument could be made, dismissing my entire point, that no one is perfect. If you or I are looking for a savior as a budo teacher, we are both in for a long search. I would not dispute that. I think, however, that begs the issue. I am not depending on a budo sensei as a role model. I do not expect him to be perfect. I am looking at him primarily as an instructor, one who possesses some skills I want and who has the ability and means to teach them. I do not have to approve of everything he does or thinks in order to learn what I want to know from him. Certainly that has been true in my case. I do not agree entirely, in terms of politics or in many other ways, with any of my sensei. I do not share all their views of life. I was sufficiently grounded by my own upbringing when I began budo that I did not need moral guides. On the other hand, there has been nothing any of my sensei have ever done that I consider to be morally repugnant. They are not perfect men. Decidedly, they are all decent men. They lead upright lives. They are honest and respectful of others. And while I did not need them as moral trailblazers, I did and do regard them—sometimes consciously, sometimes unconsciously—as role models.

I was just barely a teenager when I started budo. Those who taught me had a lot to say about the way I think men in particular and adults in general should conduct themselves. Psychologists tell us that parents carry the great bulk of responsibility in the creation of our moral character. I don't doubt that. It was so in my own upbringing. Still, we cannot ignore the influences exerted on us by athletic coaches, by school teachers, by Scout or church or community leaders who spend so much time with young people—like budo sensei. So in that sense I was fortunate. Had I been unlucky enough to have trained with teachers who were dishonest or immoral, it is possible I may have changed as a human. Budo like karate-do have had a tremendous effect on my life. The quality of those who led me would be difficult to underestimate. I am reminded of that frequently.

Just the other day I heard from a high school–age reader who asked my opinion about his continuing to train with his teacher. The teacher was dating one of the women in the dojo but was flirting, in class, with another. A vicious argument ensued between the teacher and the girlfriend, right in the middle of the training. I tried to picture any of my teachers ever doing that, under any circumstances. I could not. And I wonder if, had I had immature leadership of this sort when I was young, would I not have a different perspective on budo today. I cannot say, speaking from my own experience, whether it was good or bad for me to have to separate what a teacher *taught* from what a teacher *was,* because none of my sensei have embodied that disconnect. I am lucky. However, it also makes me a poor authority on this subject and that is why I like to ask the question to those who have had to deal with it or who might have a more enlightened perspective.

Some of the answers I have received to this question have, to some degree, been models of equivocation. Would you train with someone who was technically proficient but a lousy human being? It depends on how egregious the immoral or inappropriate behavior, some tell me. A married sensei who has had an affair with a student, regretted it, and has tried to rebuild his or her life and marriage afterward, for instance, is one thing. A sensei who indulges in serial sexual abuse with students is something else. Most of those of whom I have asked this question distinguish between mistakes we make as fallible humans and consistent, deliberate acts of depravity or crassness. I guess I would make such a distinction as well. I can say that no matter how great a sensei, no matter what his or her level of skill, there is no way I would train under a sensei who committed some acts I consider sufficiently reprehensible: sexual predation, theft, drug abuse. I suppose we all have our own standards. But if we have them, we must be absolute in applying them or they will mean nothing. These standards, I hasten to add, are applicable not exclusively to others but, by reflection, to oneself. By that, I mean that I would not want to consider as a sensei a person who was a cocaine user because, among other reasons, I would not wish my name and reputation to be associated with someone like that. Some will disagree: "I have a sensei in the dojo, just like I have a plumber in my kitchen. As long as the plumber fixes my sink and charges me fairly for it, I don't particularly care what he does elsewhere. Same with my sensei. He teaches me on the mat. What he does off it isn't any of my business." This argument is a rationalization. Your name, for better or worse, is associated with your dojo and not just for the technical teaching that goes on there. You do not get to choose who will make that association and how it will be done.

I think this matter of considering personal qualities and character as a factor in accepting or rejecting a teacher applies as well to another question I was recently asked by another reader. Perhaps my first thought by way of answer to that question might have some implications with the question before us now.

There is a martial arts teacher who claims to instruct in a *sogo budo*, a "comprehensive martial art," meaning in this case that the art contains unarmed combat methods as well as techniques with the sword and other weapons. I have seen the weaponry of this art demonstrated. It is pathetic. Obviously new-fashioned, probably from the imagination of the teacher. Still, other people whose opinions I value insist that the unarmed aspects of this art are quite good, are worth learning. The consensus is that the teacher got some instruction somewhere and he's got a real talent for improving on the basic methods he learned. He has done that, but he has also glommed on to a bunch of silly weapons stuff in the hope of giving his art some historical authenticity. I was recently asked, would I be willing, if I had a chance and the interest in learning another unarmed combat system, to become this teacher's student? Could I overlook the concocted aspects of his art to learn the good stuff? The first response that popped into my head was this: No, I would not, because if I can't believe *everything* a teacher says, I cannot believe *anything* he or she tells me.

Maybe that is too simplistic. It's easy for me to say, since I have had teachers who are good in both the technical and moral sense of that word. I could believe that anything they told me was the truth, and so I could rely on everything they said. So if you are in the position of having to make a decision of the sort we are discussing, feel free to ignore my thoughts. But please keep in mind something I said earlier. I mentioned there are not a lot of people around who I think could take me where I want to go in my pursuit of mastering karate-do or any other budo. Please think about that, about where *you* want to go in your study of karate-do or any of the martial arts. If you are clear on that, it could be you will be a lot clearer as well on exactly who it is you wish to lead you in that direction.

4

Connections

Few attributes—not enthusiasm, not good intentions, not aptitude certainly—count for so much toward making the art of karate-do a part of one's life as does consistency. It is crucial. Without it, no matter what you have going for you, no matter whether you are pursuing the Way of karate or aikido or kendo or any other of the Japanese budo, you are unlikely ever to proceed far in your journey along a martial Way.

It would not be going out on a limb to observe that the importance of consistency is a virtue essential to many other endeavors. Finishing college, dieting, creating a good marriage—in these and most other serious enterprises one must stick to it and see it through to completion if one expects to succeed. Yet a challenging budo form such as karate-do seems in some ways to epitomize the role consistency plays in meeting a goal. I believe it has something to do with the structure of the art itself: the way it is organized, taught, and learned.

When I was a beginner, I never gave much thought to the learning process of the budo I was engaged in, much less the way in which they were taught. I went to the dojo, learned, and practiced what my sensei told me or showed me. It was not until I had been doing this for some time that it occurred to me there was a kind of curriculum involved. By "curriculum," I do not mean that one learns basic punching, then more advanced methods of striking, or that a basic front kick is demonstrated, taught, and then progressively more complicated kicking skills are introduced. Yes, these progressive lessons are deliberate building blocks that provide a way to learn karate-do. I am sure you have seen what appear to be outlines of the art of karate's curriculum. If you have not, thumb through the table of contents of any of the dozens of instructional manuals devoted to it. You will see all the techniques organized in a clear and comprehensive way. Under "Stances" we find front stance, back stance, straddle-leg stance, and so on. Under "Blocks" we see listed rising block, lower block, inward block, et cetera. It might make you think you can start with the first chapter and work your way through the book and that at the end you will have gotten all that is there, all that is in the art of karate. And you're done. Underlying these lists of techniques, however, is a much more comprehensive network that would be difficult to diagram or so simply explain.

A mature and fully developed budo form such as karate-do is more than the sum of its components. There is, in addition to the curriculum of technique, a matrix that is invisible to the beginner. It appears to the more advanced practitioner only if he or she knows what to look for or, more likely, if the student has a competent teacher who can point out the right direction to look. Those of you who have been practicing karate for a while, for instance, know that the simpler (by comparison) kata of Heian or Naifanchi are taught before learning the more complex forms of say, Bassai or Kanku-dai. It makes sense. But why, in those forms of karate-do that teach them both, is the kata Gankaku introduced before Jion? Or Hangetsu taught before Empi? (I am using examples of kata taught by the Japan Karate Association [JKA] here; practitioners of other styles of karate will recognize other names perhaps, though they should see, if they are being taught properly, that their system has its own generally fixed order in which all kata are introduced.)

One can make the argument successfully and accurately that the Heian kata are shorter or simpler or more modern and therefore more suited to beginners than are older and more complicated forms such as Bassai or Kanku-dai. It is a good and obvious point and has some validity. That argument loses some of its power of persuasion when one tries to understand why older and longer forms, which are equal to each other in their age and complexity, are still taught in a specific order. Some more experienced kareteka exponents will, at this point, be a bit smug, thinking they know the answer. And they may, to some degree. They will tell you that the reason, for instance, Sochin and Hangetsu are taught quickly, one right after the other, is that Sochin strengthens the outer musculature while Hangetsu works to build the inner, contracting actions of the body. About the time the typical JKA student reaches his nidan (second degree black belt), he or she can appreciate the distinct kinds of body dynamics featured in these kata and so can manipulate the kata to best effect in building his or her body. They will be able to explain that the light, quick movements of Empi must be countered by the heavier and more slowly rhythmic actions of Jutte.

These answers to why the kata are taught in a particular order are not incorrect. But they are also far from complete. There is a deeper mechanism working here. The individual kata are taught in a specific sequence because each of them presents, in unique ways, individual challenges for the karateka studying them. And the solution to each challenge provides the means necessary to meet the following one. They are interconnected. The same, not incidentally, is true for the kata of the various systems of *iaido* (sword drawing). It is also true for the formal kata of judo, for those noble and solitary few *judoka* out there who still have the brains and fortitude to study them. The kata of most, if not all, budo forms are like interlocking clues to a puzzle, if I may greatly simplify. You solve this kind of puzzle by beginning at the beginning and working your way through it. In others words, it will not help you a bit to have clue 6 before you find and understand the ramifications of clues 5 and 4 before that. You cannot skip ahead. You cannot, to look at it another way, see all of the layers of an onion unless you peel off each layer, one at a time. Most important, you must be consistent in your practice. You may believe you can cut through some of the layers or tear off several at a time. It will not work. You must stick to it, consistently, week after week, year after year, step by step.

I suspect most karate students are little different than I was when they were beginners like me. The amount of material seemed vast enough in itself. Just memorizing the sequences in a long kata, trying to keep the kata separate, remembering all the technical details of dozens of different techniques—it is overwhelming. Once, one of my sensei took pity on me when I began one kata and somehow diverted into another before my entire performance dissolved into a meandering barrage of punches. I stood in the middle of the dojo, lost as if I had been blindfolded and dropped off in the middle of the Amazon Basin. My sensei laughed. He explained that he had been training himself for about ten years before, as he put it, he "learned how to learn." At the time I thought the comment facile. I wanted to learn as quickly as possible and as much as possible. In addition to practice at the dojo I read everything I could find on karate-do. I asked questions constantly. I was like an engineer putting the wires in the right connections on a circuit board or some other complex piece of technology. Each time I found where the end of one wire fit, I looked to see where the other might go. When I found the connection, I was delighted. I did not realize then that there might be more than one way the wires might be configured, that in reality the sophistication of karate's circuit board allowed for a nearly infinite variety in those possible connections. (I know, I am playing fast and loose with analogies here, comparing karate to an onion in one paragraph and to a bit of computer technology in the next. It is not easy to describe the process. Analogies, however inadequate, are useful in approaching it.) It was only after I had been at karate for those ten years that I had some basic idea of the layout of the entire board. I did not know where all the wires went. Yet I knew vaguely what the board looked like. Making the connections became more interesting and simultaneously more intriguing. It is a process that continues for me, as it does for all serious karateka, even today.

At this point, I suspect there are some readers who are concerned that I am revealing too much. These are matters that must be introduced by the teacher and that must be pursued by students themselves. The student will receive some hints and a lot of encouragement from the sensei. He or she must, however, solve the puzzle, or, more accurately, the puzzles, alone. Or peel the onion. Or wire the circuit board. I suspect, too, that there are some "sensei" out there also who are gritting their teeth, irritated that I am not going further into this subject, because after their students read this, they will approach their teachers, asking for answers about some of these connections. At this point, these self-promoted experts are going to have to come up with some fast answers. (Here's a hint for those of you who have convinced others, even yourself perhaps, that you are fully matured as a teacher and can lead others: when the students start asking you about these connections in the kata, just try your best to smile enigmatically and say something like "Ah, you are too impatient. Study harder and all will be revealed!" Good luck. Students might believe you really do know and aren't just putting them off. Then again, students are getting smarter these days, aren't they?)

I am not trying to tease the serious reader here, dangling a carrot of information and then snatching it away without giving you a taste. Instead, I am trying to introduce an idea to your training that may not have occurred to you before. I hope you will begin to see some connections that you may not have noticed previously. This is a subject in which answers cannot be given out easily. It is not that the "secrets" cannot be revealed. It is that the secrets are highly individual. I am still discovering them for myself, just as you will if your training is consistent and dedicated.

5

Do You Need to Go to Japan?

It is the question that must be posed internally, or among one's dojomates, by every karateka who has gone much past the stage one learns to tie the belt correctly. Is it necessary to go to Japan to become the best karate practitioner I can be? Is it worthwhile to go to Japan? And if so, why? Of course, there are those karate schools so far removed from the roots of their arts that practitioners in them may assume karate was invented in southern California back about the time the Beatles first came to America. Most karate students, I am hoping, will know that karate-do originated on the archipelago of Okinawa and was developed in a number of different ways after some iterations of it were brought to mainland Japan in the early twentieth century. Along with geisha and Godzilla, karate may be among the first things the average person thinks of when Japan is mentioned. So naturally, those who become active practitioners sooner or later contemplate making a trip to the "homeland" of their art, either to train or to get a sense of the culture that spawned it.

Let's establish first that when we talk about karate's "homeland," we are oversimplifying things. Today, Okinawa is a prefecture of Japan. It was annexed in the early seventeenth century after many centuries of independence as an island kingdom. We are apt to think of Okinawa as little more than the southernmost reach of Japan. In truth, there are significant differences between Okinawan culture and the culture of mainland Japan. This is evident in the different ways in which karate is practiced in both places. As I said, we often think of karate as essentially "Japanese." Many Okinawans object to this. Some insist the Japanese do not even understand karate at all and that, indeed, understanding it is impossible without speaking and comprehending the Okinawan dialect. The mentality of the Okinawan karateka was historically different from that of the Japanese martial artist. There are reverberations of that remaining today, as anyone who has trained in karate in both places can tell you. In some ways, the differences between Okinawan karate and the Japanese versions of it can be as distinctive as the differences found in the art as popularly practiced in the West. I am not trying to downplay or ignore these distinctions when I am talking about "going to Japan." I am not implying that traveling to Tokyo to study one's karate is no different from going to a dojo in Naha, Okinawa. I think, though, that the points that follow will be true for both destinations.

There are many ways of looking at this matter of going to Japan to further one's karate in terms of coming to a personal answer. My own perspective is to compare going to Japan to polish or refine one's karate training with the experience of going to, say, Italy, to further one's culinary abilities in Italian cuisine. I can follow recipes for a lot of Italian dishes. I can even experiment a little and have my own take on several. I am interested in Italian cooking in a sort of superficial way. In no way could I be considered an expert or even well informed about the subtleties or range of Italian cuisine. I am content with that. On the other hand, if I wanted to become an authority on Italian cooking, to understand it in its cultural perspective, then I would begin by learning Italian and by exploring the culture of the country. I would go to where Italian cuisine originated to advance and expand my knowledge.

My approach would be more scholarly and more serious if I wanted to really understand the full range, depths, and dimensions of Italian food and cooking. True, there are a lot of good Italian cookbooks around. There are experts in the art in this country to whom I could go and take classes. I could go to work in an Italian restaurant of the sort that we have in the thousands here in the United States. Even so, there are lessons to be learned in a country kitchen in the rural backwaters of Tuscany that I cannot learn from a book or even from firsthand instruction by teachers in this country. There are dishes that can only be mastered when the oregano in that dish is snipped from a bush in the cook's garden. There are lessons that can only be absorbed in the place where that food originated. But before signing up for Italian classes or getting my passport stamped for Rome, I need to be clear on why I am going. Is learning all of that, at that depth and breadth, really important enough to me to take on such travel? Or do I just want to be able to whip up, when the mood strikes, a nice meal of *pasta con broccoli*? That is the same sort of question that needs to be asked by the karateka contemplating a stay in Japan. How deep and how wide does one wish to go? Or can afford to make, in terms of other aspects of his or her life—school, job or career, family commitments?

There are some fundamental, prosaic considerations. Living in another country is usually expensive. It is exorbitantly so, or can be, in Japan. Cost is no small factor in your decision. There are hundreds and hundreds of young karateka, fresh out of high school, who decide to go off to Japan to live for a year or so, to practice and polish their karate. Many assume they will be able to find a job and a place to stay, that it will just all happen, a happy, felicitous denouement to this chapter in their life because they are, after all, sincere and determined. It sounds nice but it rarely works. Several companies offer jobs in Japan teaching English that seem perfect. In some cases these opportunities turn out well. In others, applicants fail to read all the fine print. Once in Japan, they find themselves teaching several classes a day, in multiple locations. They are so busy with this work and commuting that there is no time for karate training. Housing and food can also be so expensive it is impossible to pay dues at the dojo. And landlords routinely refuse to rent to foreigners in Japan. Even a routine illness like a cold can sap energy and enthusiasm. What was to be a grand experience ends with the intrepid visitor huddled under a cheap blanket, sniffling and miserable, in a drafty, three-mat apartment that is sucking the warmth out of a portable heater almost as fast as the rent is being sucked from his rapidly thinning savings. It is depressing, yes. But if you are contemplating a long stay in Japan, you must be certain you have the finances and the possibility of a suitable job *before* you board the jet.

Before addressing the question of whether one should travel to Japan or not, the karate student needs to be clear on why he or she is training. If his interest in karate is because it is a challenging sport or avenue for physical fitness, or if he enjoys seeing how high he can reach in a ranking system, there is no reason to go to Japan. There are many opportunities to participate in sporting events related to karate in this country, to practice it as part of a fitness regime, and to achieve rank. The time and expense of going to Japan—at least in the interest of furthering one's karate—is not really worthwhile for that person.

This will discomfit many, but in my opinion, technically speaking, there are several Western karate teachers whose talents and ability to instruct are every bit as good as any karate sensei I have seen in Japan. (The Western teachers may, in some ways, be better, simply because in sharing a common language and culture, the student and teacher do not have so much getting in the way of their communicating.) If you are interested in perfecting your karate skills from a purely technical level, learning from one of these teachers is an obvious way to go. There is no magic in the air of a Japanese karate dojo. There are no secrets to be whispered in your ear by a Japanese karate teacher in Japan that will miraculously improve your inside forearm block. I think on some level most of us know this. Still, there is a sense among many karateka that they will gain a special insight into their karate if they go to Japan. It is as if their kata will somehow be refined by practicing it in front of a Buddhist temple or in a Japanese dojo. If you are one of them, prepare for disappointment. Hundreds of martial artists of all kinds have gone to Japan only to discover that training in their own dojo back in Ohio or Florida actually is more productive. There have been some bitter souls on homeward flights leaving Tokyo, martial artists who spent large sums of money, gave up good jobs, or postponed their education, all in the belief a trip to Japan would be something that it was not.

All that said, why *would* you need a trip to Japan to become a better karateka? Let's go back to my analogy of Italian cooking. There are people who are far more passionate about mastering Italian cuisine than am I. They want to know it, to understand it not just from a technical perspective, but from a historical and cultural perspective as well. For these sorts, Italy is an obvious and necessary destination. Karate-do is no different. Are you interested in karate's native culture? Do you want to see how it developed and evolved within a society? Then you must go to that culture, to that society.

Let's be clear: if you are training here under a good, qualified instructor, your punches will be no faster and no stronger as a result of going to Japan. Good, qualified karate teachers are difficult to find, that is true. But they are here. They are all over the world. And they can teach you as well as anyone in Japan, in terms of polishing and perfecting technique. They can teach you about the correct spirit of karate.

What you will get from going to Japan is largely intangible. The benefits accrue incrementally. It is not some big awakening. It is more a sense of little things clicking into place: "oh, so that's why we do this in the dojo." You will see connections between Japanese culture and karate that are subtle yet often profound. You will see karate-do and other budo within the context of the culture in which they were spawned. That is no small factor in learning to appreciate these arts fully.

6

Rank, or Lack Thereof

A friend, a longtime practitioner of one of Japan's oldest classical martial arts, was asked how best to explain what it is like to join a traditional *ryu*, or hereditary school devoted to these arts. "Tell them, 'Welcome to the ryu,'" he said, "then add: 'You're never going anywhere.'"

There is a certain degree of cynicism in the comment. It does, though, put into perspective a reality of training in one of the feudal-era arts of Japan's past. What he meant was that in the ryu of which he was a member, as in many other ryu devoted to these ancient schools that continue to exist today, the innermost secrets of the art are reserved for a very few. In the case of the ryu he joined some years ago—more appropriate to say the one where he was accepted—the *gokui kaiden*, or "transmission of the secrets," is reserved for only one or two people of each generation. They become, in effect, the "keepers of the torch," which they are expected to pass along in their own time to the next generation. It isn't that those who do not possess these final secrets are not competent in the ryu. They develop, if the ryu has been correctly preserved and passed on, remarkable skills and insights. The *gokui*, or "secrets," of the ryu tend to have more to do with esoteric teachings than with practical applications. Virtually all classical ryu have these gokui. It does not matter whether the ryu is devoted to martial arts or flower arranging or calligraphy or any other of the arts that are preserved and passed on through the ryu system. In most instances the secrets are not necessary for physical, technical competence. Instead, they encapsulate the essence of what animates the ryu and gives it its essential character. In some cases the gokui may be one or two kata that are a distillate of all that has been taught, a way of ultimately "summing up" the techniques. In other ryu, the exclusive secrets will be devotional exercises aimed at some Buddhist or Shinto deity who is central to the heritage of the art. My friend's point was that since these gokui are passed on only to the next chosen headmaster, the average person enters this particular school knowing with reasonable certainty that he or she will never reach the end of things.

For some, I suspect this might be maddening. They would equate it to entering a college knowing that no matter how hard they study, how broad their participation, they will never graduate. Or it would be like joining a sports team with the knowledge that your team will never win a championship. Never to reach what seems to be the logical conclusion of an art makes a pursuit of it appear a waste of time. Consider, though, another way of thinking about it: When you enter a marriage, do you expect to receive sometime in your future a certificate or a "rank" that acknowledges how good you will eventually have become at marriage? If you belong to an organized religion, do you get ranked in it? Or graduate? Is there an end to one's participation in these?

I mention this in regard to the enormous popularity of the *dan-i* ranking system that pervades karate-do and all the modern budo of Japan. The dan-i system is almost entirely modern in concept. Ranks, in the form of colored belts or certificates or diplomas, are issued by the dojo or the organization. As I will discuss further in chapter 14, the system was devised largely by the founder of judo, Jigoro Kano, near the end of the nineteenth century. Colored belts like we use in karate-do today were also an inspiration taken by the judo teacher Mikonosuke Kawaishi, who introduced the art in France. They are a fundamental aspect of judo, karate-do, aikido, and so on. (Kendo uses the dan-i system as well, though without the use of colored belts.) We can scarcely imagine those arts without their belt ranks. But what if we did? What would change, about the budo and about participation in them?

First, I am not much of a critic of the dan-i system of awarding ranks. I think it gets a lot of unfair criticism by people who think of themselves as traditionalists. They like to posture and opine that "ranks don't mean anything" and suggest their own involvement in the budo is above such mundane considerations. These sorts of comments have a lofty air about them and they may be sincere. They are insulting, though, to the founders of the budo they are practicing. Funakoshi, Kano, Morihei Ueshiba; all of these men either designed or specifically approved a system of ranks. If you want to study karate-do, you do not have the right to pick and choose which parts you will study and which parts you will reject. Belt ranks are a long-established part of the training in the karate dojo. If you want to train there, accept that. I once had a brief but I hope informative conversation with a young man who had just been promoted to *shodan,* the first of the black-belt ranks. I was visiting in the dojo where he had tested for the grade.

"I don't deserve this," he told me, shaking his head. He was sincere in his sentiment, I am certain, and a certain amount of humility is always nice to see. On the other hand, making too big a fuss of one's unworthiness is, if you think about it, not all that different from making a big deal out of how wonderful one is. A shrunken, misshapen ego is not substantially different from one bloated out of proportion. Neither one is healthy.

"So, it is your position that those guys over there"— I pointed to the group of senior instructors who had conducted the test and who were his teachers—"don't know as much as you do about your technique?"

"Well, no, that's not what I'm saying at all . . ." He mumbled a bit. I could see, though, that a light went on. My point was made. If he didn't deserve his promotion, he would not have gotten it and if he didn't trust the judgment of his teachers, he had no business training with them. Humility is not best expressed by critiquing, even obliquely, those who have recognized one's accomplishments.

Of course, it is true that this system is open to abuse. It is hard to argue with the sad fact that some budo teachers have manipulated belt ranks in all sorts of disreputable ways: holding them out or giving them as rewards, like the proverbial carrot on a stick; charging all sorts of excessive fees, for the testing itself or for registering the rank with the headquarters of the art in Japan; revoking them for various reasons.

Without arguing for the moment about the historical component of the ranking system in the budo or its misapplications, however, it is worthwhile simply to consider a scenario where it did not exist. To be sure, in most of our activities, even important and special ones, we do not get ranked. It would be rather odd if you were awarded a rank based on your abilities as a parent, for instance. Or as a neighbor. We tend to think of these parts of our lives as not really amenable to an objective grading system. They are responsibilities and roles we take on and we go about them on a daily basis, sometimes living up to our expectations and goals, and sometimes failing. But only under the most dire of circumstances would we consider abandoning our roles as parents or friends, even if we do not have a clear picture of exactly how we are doing at them at any one point in our lives.

A few years ago, I was determined to improve my aerobic fitness by bicycle riding. There are a series of trails with beautiful scenery only blocks from my home, and a training partner gave me a frightfully expensive bike at an incredibly generous bargain price. So I was off. For the first few months, I simply rode for an hour. After that, when I took my bike in for a tune-up, I was seduced into buying and mounting on my bike a gizmo that would tell me my speed, my average speed for that ride, and the number of miles I'd ridden that day, as well as for the entire season. In some ways, that gizmo changed my world. "I did fifteen miles in one hour yesterday; can I beat that today?" I would ask myself. At the end of the season, when it became too cold to continue riding, I noted how many miles I'd done overall for the year. And the next spring I set about to see if I could break that mileage. Runners and other athletes who participate in sports where this sort of objective analysis are common will take all this for granted. People like me, however, whose primary physical activity has always been a budo form, are apt to find it a unique experience.

We are, from a practical standpoint, largely unable to measure our progress accurately or our lack of it in karate-do. Is your reverse punch "better" than it was a year ago? How do you know? Is your kata improved? Sure, you get vague clues. I do not fall down at that part of this kata as I once did. I have at least memorized the correct sequence of techniques in that kata. When I first punched the makiwara with a reverse punch, my wrist collapsed. It does not do that anymore—at least, not so often. Once we are past the basics of things, though, that kind of measurement is tougher to make in the dojo. There isn't any gadget I can mount on my belt that will tell me how strong my kick was this week so I can compare it to last week's.

The best way we have of measuring ourselves is through the ranking system. My karate is better this year than it was last year because I have a different color on my belt that indicates it. Of course, most readers will see the problem here. First, ranking systems and requirements are so numerous and so varied that any objectivity is impossible. It is possible, we tell ourselves after our successful test for brown belt, that Sensei gave me that rank more as a reward for effort than for actual improvement. Or we suspect we might have been given that rank because the school is losing students and our teacher wants to encourage us to stay. A common criticism of the dan-i belt rank system is that it creates a false sense of accomplishment. I have a feeling, though, that just as often, it does the opposite. It causes us to doubt our worthiness or the motivations of our teacher in awarding the rank.

That's why I think it is a good idea to keep the place of the ranking system in an appropriate perspective. Take the tests, try your hardest, accept the results. But ask yourself from time to time: What would I be doing if there were no ranks in my dojo? Would I train as hard? Would I be as content? Consider your karate not as a series of steps that are symbolized by a rainbow of belts. Think of it instead as a way of life, one that is going to continue, like other important parts of your life, whether the product can be measured or not.

7

Find Out for Yourself

If you have trained in a Japanese karate dojo, or in one anywhere else in the world that has been heavily influenced by traditional Japanese culture, you will not need to be told that your personal input into things is not high on the list of necessities in your learning. You may have all sorts of wonderful ideas, what you consider to be valuable contributions and insights, your own personal take on matters. Nobody cares. Quite the opposite. The fastest way to alienate yourself in a dojo is to make known these ideas or to volunteer your suggestions on how training might be better or more effective.

Karate-do is by no means the exception in this attitude about the correct way of imparting and mastering an art, not within the Japanese model at least. The entire basis of learning in a traditional Japanese mode is approached through a willingness to submit, to embrace the lessons without criticism or personal interpretation. It does not matter the art. Enter a school for classical Japanese painting and you will find your brush soon at work on *funponshugi,* the laborious process of tracing or copying paintings from previous generations of the school. You do not create your own, original paintings for a long time. You simply copy those of others. Join a school for the tea ceremony and you will be handling the scoop or the whisk exactly as your teacher demonstrates. If you have any ideas for doing it differently you will, if you are smart, keep them to yourself. Commence karate training at the dojo and you do an elbow strike their way. And they are not interested in your insights on the strike as you may have read about doing it or the way you saw it at another dojo or as you think it might be more effective.

Certainly that was my experience when I began following the Way of karate, back in the late 1960s. Fortunately for me, I began karate when public information about it in the West was limited. Unlike today, when people can see it in videos, TV programs, and movies, when I began I had never seen karate other than in books and magazines. So I did not have a lot of ideas of any sort. It did not take me too long to learn that even if I did, they were not particularly welcome. "Shut up and follow the model" was the way my teachers taught. So I did. It was not easy. I am opinionated and have my own thoughts on things, just as most of us do. I often had to grit my teeth. For the most part, I was successful. My ability to adapt to this form of learning was not, I hasten to add, from any great perceptive powers or cultural sensitivity I might have. It was more from fear. I saw what happened to other people when they tried to make their opinions or ideas known. They were either humiliated or ignored. Avoiding that sort of thing was a powerful incentive to me, a young teenager. One of the first expressions I learned in Japanese refers to the image of a nailed surface like a shingled roof where one of the nails has worked its way up and out of the wood. "The nail that sticks out gets pounded back down." *Kugi wa tsukidashi.* I didn't want to be that *kugi,* that nail. So I kept my mouth shut and I followed the instructions of my sensei.

Eventually, they introduced me to karate-do's *mawashi-geri,* or roundhouse kick. For some time I had been working on its mechanics. Eventually, I noticed the foot of my supporting leg behaved differently depending on which was my kicking foot. Kicking with the right leg, my left, supporting foot twisted out as soon as I lifted the right leg. Kicking with my left leg, my right, supporting foot twisted around later, just as the kick made contact.

Discrepancies in our supposedly bilateral movements are not uncommon, of course. Soccer players always favor one leg over the other. Next time you are standing and putting on a pair of socks, pay close attention and you will see that putting on the left and right are not mirror movements. Your body adjusts in subtle ways depending on which side you use. Often these anomalies are caused by skeletal or muscular differences. Many people have one leg shorter than the other, for instance. Our muscular system develops to compensate. But it produces differences between left and right, as it did in my roundhouse kicks. What I wanted to know was not what caused it, but rather, which way was more effective. Was it better to turn the supporting foot out as the kicking leg chambered? Or wait until the moment of contact with the target? I asked one of my sensei. His answer surprised me.

"Find out for yourself."

Wait a minute, I thought. For months and months now, I have been told precisely how to make every movement. Intense scrutiny has been given to the degree to which my thumb ought to be cocked when making a knife-hand strike; which toes I should squeeze as I step forward has been explained, again and again. And then again. I have been working like a fiend trying to avoid being that nail that sticks out. Now, all of a sudden, I am just supposed to figure this out on my own? Take initiative? Stick out?

Critics of the traditional method of teaching frequently target the precise—and let's face it, *"precise"* is a polite term; *"nitpicky"* might be a better one—exactness that often seems to belabor every karate class. They note, correctly to some extent, the preoccupation with getting every little detail exactly right—sometimes, it seems, to the detriment of effectiveness. Knock a guy out with a single punch and nevertheless the sensei is admonishing you because your back foot was turned at 49 degrees and it should have been at 45 degrees. Soar through the air with the majestic grace of an eagle, your side kick flashing out to stop just a fraction of an inch from your opponent's jaw, and the sensei criticizes you because your big toe was not properly cocked. Yes, there is an aesthetic element to karate-do. Critics observe, though, that when aesthetics outweigh practical results, the art becomes foppish and contrived. It's more about image than substance. These are legitimate observations to some extent.

What critics don't stick around long enough to see, however, is that the near-obsessive attention to detail is part of the *process* of developing a student. It is one step in their progression, not the end product. Critics who do not spend a lot of time in the dojo do not see that process as it matures. They do not see the part of training where the student is expected to begin to figure it out on his or her own.

The truth is that training in a traditional Japanese way is always a path filled with enormous tension. Students must be willing to submit, to sublimate ego and ideas. But they never succeed entirely—unless they are some kind of automaton. And ironically, the teacher does not wish them to be. It is not an extinguishing of personal will or creativity the teacher is seeking. Instead, the teacher wants that will and creative spirit to be fully developed. Think of it this way: You may be living next to a lake. All those millions of gallons of water, however, are useless to you in putting out your house fire unless they can be channeled and propelled correctly with a hose. One's talent and creativity are useless, according to this manner of teaching and learning, unless they are channeled effectively. It is this constant tension, between adhering to form and learning to express oneself, that provides much of the dynamic of real teaching and learning in karate-do or any other budo.

The tension I am talking about is not an abstraction. It is real and incredibly powerful. The beginner is not usually aware of it.

Like me when I began, if one is really interested in learning, one looks around, sees how it goes in this place, and follows along. Later, though, the dynamic tension between a karateka and the sensei becomes dramatic, even if it is never openly expressed. The karateka is maturing, like an adolescent who was content yesterday to obey the 10 P.M. curfew set by her parents but who, a day later, starts asking why she can't stay out until midnight. Push this too far, she knows, and she risks being grounded. But she is aching to stay out later. Her parents know why the push is on and they know that, eventually, they will have to accept a child capable of staying out past the evening news. But how much they give and when they give it, how much and how quickly the child asks and demands, that is the stuff of growing up. Arguments, sullen obedience, tears and resentment: it is no different in the dojo. Yes, I was allowed a limited freedom in exploring the best way to do the roundhouse kick. Had I decided I was equally free to be creative, exploring variations in other areas of training, I'd have been pounded down quickly.

Interestingly, teachers in some Japanese arts distinguish between what is produced through our own creativity and what comes through following the set form. Kano Yasunobu (1613–1685) was one of the great masters of the Kano school of formal painting. In his treatise *Gado Yoketsu* (The Secret Art of Painting) he distinguishes between *shitsuga,* or works produced through innate ability, and *gakuga,* or those paintings created through the formal process of training in the school. Kano notes that teachers should recognize the former, without praising them or making a big deal about them. Why? The answer is very important. Because while these paintings may demonstrate creativity and skill, those talents cannot be taught and passed on. They arise in certain individuals for reasons no one knows. They are not reliably transmittable. The teacher recognizes that the student will either have some innate talent or they will not. It is not the job of the teacher to develop that individual talent within the student. It is the task of the teacher to instill correct form, to create a physical environment in which that talent, if there is any, can be exercised and perfected in a positive way.

The whole process of kata—and it is kata around which *all* arts taught within the structure of Japanese tradition are taught—is to build a foundation. As that foundation is being built, and particularly after it has been constructed, the student has to experiment to see what and how to build on top of it or within it. We are all unique. The teaching methods employed by Japanese arts are not so simplistic or so autocratic as not to recognize this obvious fact. They simply take a different approach in nurturing our unique characteristics. My teachers gave me a good, solid foundation in making a roundhouse kick. They taught me the basics and insisted I follow them uncritically. At the correct time, as they did in the case of my question, they also gave me insight into the nature of our art. As I was to hear many, many times again and still do today, and as you will yourself hear if you have a good teacher, "find out for yourself."

8

Pace

Within all the martial arts of Japan, practitioners speak of three elements that are critical in fighting. *Choshi, hyoshi,* and *ma no tori-kata* are often cited as essentials in combat strategy. Each one of these is worthy of years of intense study. They are best learned, however, as integral parts of a whole. *Hyoshi* refers to the "timing" in an encounter. Timing in this sense is the "beat." A boxer rattling a speed bag is a study in good hyoshi. If he or she loses the beat, the bag will wobble or go off at an angle and the punches will not connect properly. Lose the beat and you lose the flow.

Ma no tori-kata is the efficient use of the *ma* or "space" between opponents. This space will change radically, constantly, depending on factors such as the weapons one or both participants may be wielding or the ground on which they are fighting. Manipulating the space to best advantage between oneself and one's opponent, whether that space or interval is at a distance or close up, is a function of this element of strategy. A karateka who can be equally effective at five feet or at only inches from an opponent has a mastery of using the interval of space that separates him from his target, whatever that space is. That is a big advantage to have in combat. In the thirties and forties in Japan when karate schools began sparring with one another, either as official events or by students on the sly wishing to try their stuff against someone outside the dojo, the element of ma no tori-kata became prominent in karate. Different dojo and different kinds of karate found they had become comfortable with a specific spacing between partners. Suddenly they were faced with opponents who may have had another preference for spacing. Karateka accustomed to the wide interval necessary to unleash a long, looping kick were taken by surprise when they were nose to nose with an attacker. Karateka who were comfortable fighting with their knees nearly touching had a lot of trouble dealing with an attack that was launched from several feet away.

Choshi is trickier to translate than the other two. It is often rendered as "rhythm." That is not a bad way to describe it; perhaps, for our discussion, "pace" might be a better way to think of choshi. We might also distinguish between hyoshi and choshi this way: If I punch at your face and you wait until just before my attack lands, then you shift so I miss and you can launch a counterattack, you are using a particular form of hyoshi, or timing. That is the same timing we mentioned earlier, with the boxer and his speed bag. Choshi, though, rather than describing one encounter or one exercise, concerns the overall rhythm of a fight. Just as a piece of music might contain more than one beat in its composition, a fight might have varied timing as it unfolds, sometimes quick, at other times slow. The choshi is the overall pace that includes all those different timings.

As you undoubtedly know, every fight or confrontation has its own pace. It does not matter whether the confrontation is a cop arresting a belligerent drunk at the corner bar or a war of global proportions. There is antagonism, confrontation, and resolution in each situation and in every one of any size or consequences in between. Sportive approaches to karate are often characterized by their pace, in fact. If the match is between two relatively inexperienced practitioners, then one of them, usually the more aggressive one, will set the pace of the fight. He will be bouncing around out of range, then closing, then pulling back, on and on, and the other contestant will tend to follow his pacing. Due to his inexperience, however, the guy setting the pace doesn't know how to make best use of it. He may back out or slow things down if he is tired or nervous. He is controlling the pace, but not the fight. When one opponent is more skilled, he deliberately sets this rhythm or pace and takes advantage of it. Even if his opponent is attacking, the person with the superior ability at setting the pace will be in control of the fight.

One of the more worthwhile exercises for the serious karateka is to observe the rhythms or pace of other forms of combat. Or even other kinds of movement. Too many karate-do practitioners never watch a tae kwon do match, or a fencing bout, or a round of boxing. It is to their detriment for many reasons, not the least being that it prevents them from learning to spot and counter or take advantage of different kinds of choshi. The pace of *muay Thai*, for example, is much different from that of a karate match. In muay Thai, Thailand's famous fighting art, battles tend to start out slowly and then gradually increase in speed. The rhythms are at first relaxed and cautious. The two fighters in the opening round are feeling one another out. As the rounds go on, the pace increases. The choshi of a muay Thai fight in the middle rounds sometimes looks nearly frantic. Indeed, the method for scoring in muay Thai is actually devised to encourage this pace, with more points being given for good technique in the later rounds that in those earlier in the fight. That's why the fourth round of the traditional five-round bout is called the "money round" in the sport. Western-style boxing tends to begin in a similar fashion, with the boxers trying to get a sense of their opponents. In later rounds, they tend to be more aware of the scoring. Their corner men will let them know if they are ahead or behind, and they try to adjust the pace to that.

Real combative engagements between two people—fights

"for real"—tend to have a much less predictable rhythm. Back in the early 1960s, when yakuza criminals in Japan were at their most violent, their attacks were characterized by a sudden, explosive charge, usually with a knife or short sword. These wild assaults were almost never carried out against non-yakuza. They were fights between different yakuza families or clans. So the expectation was that your enemy suspected you were coming. He was prepared and he was willing, and you knew, as a fellow yakuza, to equal your attack or to escalate matters. Further, the police could be expected to intervene if a fight lasted too long. So things had to be brutal, decisive, and quick. The attackers in a yakuza assault were not particularly skillful. But they came rushing at an opponent unexpectedly, going from stillness to frenzied action in an eyeblink, flailing like a windmill with the blade. Yakuza assaults of this sort set a pace that was difficult to defend or organize against.

We now have gangs of young thugs in urban areas around the world who employ a different pace in their attacks in two- or three-on-one confrontations. The thugs will gather, standing on a street corner and suddenly jacking an innocent bystander so quickly and from such an odd angle that a defense is unlikely. The intent may be robbery, or it may also be for the sheer, predatory thrill of it. It is informative to watch some of the videos of these vicious and senseless attacks, by the way. If you do, you will see the attacker rarely puts himself in position to make a follow-up move. He hopes the surprise and the force of his initial strike will incapacitate the victim. Since he has usually chosen a victim who does not present much of a formidable presence, this method has a good chance of succeeding. Watch, however, videos of similar ambush attacks by and against convicts in prison exercise yards and you will see just the opposite. The attacker assumes his victim will be able to organize his body and put up a secondary defense after the initial assault. Consequently, the assailant rushes the victim and keeps hitting or stabbing or kicking, just as the yakuza did.

Few fights begin utterly spontaneously. There is almost always an overall pace to events, even if we cannot detect it. I am thinking, for example, of a soldier sneaking up on a sentry from behind and suddenly strangling him, killing him almost instantly. Where is the choshi in that "fight"? Some of us would say there was none, particularly those whose view of combat is confined to face-to-face encounters. Strategists from Sun Tzu to Yagyu Munenori to modern experts on warfare and combat, though, would discern a subtle rhythm and pace to events that would or should be detectable to the skilled warrior. Was the weather amenable for a sneak attack against the sentry? Was the enemy strong enough or desperate enough to try such a tactic? Knowing these rhythms has always been a part of warfare. In some ways, the art of war can be thought of as an art of choshi.

Fights in our world usually begin with a discernible pace, if you think about it or know what to look for. You cut me off in traffic. I follow and jump out of my car at the next light. I approach and the verbal exchanges lead to moving into position on both our parts and then maybe there is a shove or a punch—all of these are a continuing escalation of violence and all as well have a place in the determination of the rhythm of the encounter. I once heard a good story about a martial artist in a corner of a public park, warming up and waiting for his classmates to arrive for an outdoor practice. A car pulled up near him; its occupants began taunting. They were—this is one way of looking at it—setting a pace, prepared for it to escalate. The martial artist confounded them very cleverly. He simply stood there and looked at them. He refused to respond to the pace they were trying to set, and in doing so, his command and control of the pace of their exchange stymied them. The only way they could regain it would be to approach him. Since he was holding a weapon, or perhaps because they did not really want a physical confrontation, they were not eager to do that. He stood and looked and did nothing. Eventually, they probably felt a little stupid and drove away. His use of choshi was exceptional.

Interestingly, choshi and hyoshi are not at all confined to a study of fighting arts. They are terms readily familiar to traditional Japanese musicians who perform *gagaku* (ancient court music, consisting of strange old instruments and weird chanting) or *taiko* drumming or who play other traditional instruments. The great figure of the Noh theater, Zeami, who was a friend of many warriors including Yagyu Munenori, noted that pacing in the art of Noh is a critical skill for the actor. His words on mastering pacing in the movements of a drama were to "carry the body in accordance with the various circumstances and the action will come of itself." According to legend, when Yagyu Munenori, the founder of his family's school of swordsmanship, heard Zeami's advice, he clapped his hands and exclaimed, "That is the essence of swordsmanship; that is the essence of a victorious strategy." Zeami probably never held a sword; certainly he knew nothing of swordsmanship or martial arts. But he knew choshi, and knew it well.

9

Buji Kore Kaere Meiba

Buji kore kaere meiba is an old expression that comes from the feudal era in Japan. "It's a noteworthy horse that can return its rider to safety" is a rough translation. The epigram was coined during the times when battle was joined and fought to some extent by cavalry, and having a horse that could transport its rider away from a battle was almost as important as having one that could get its rider into the action. In modern, colloquial Japanese, the expression survives. It is sometimes used as a way of saying that everything's all right because everyone made it home safely. It is a sort of Japanese version of "all's well that ends well."

Horses have never been plentiful in Japan. Horses required a lot of open range with plenty of grasses and grains. Fields that would have been needed for pasturing the animals were more productively used for growing rice and the other sorts of grains and plants needed for human consumption. Distances in Japan, even from one end of the country to the other, are not all that excessive. It is a collection of small islands, after all. And so the comparatively rapid transportation provided by a horse was not enough of an advantage in daily life or in military campaigns for them to be raised in great numbers. Consequently—if you have seen authentic depictions of samurai battle in movies you will have noted this—while upper-ranked samurai often led horseback charges into battle, the majority of the fighting was carried out by foot soldiers. Even though an old term for "martial arts" in Japanese is *kyuba michi* or "the Way of the horse and bow," as warfare developed in Japan the role of the mounted warrior was a less and less significant factor in tactics. Even in many classical martial arts devoted to the preservation of ancient combat, the lessons and teachings of fighting on horseback have either been lost or discarded over the centuries from lack of use.

It is too bad in a way that we do not know a lot about the methods of mounted combat in ancient Japan. Such knowledge and skills would have little relevancy in the modern world, to be sure. The more technical understanding we have of warfare and fighting in the past, though, the better we can understand the mentalities and sensibilities of people in other times. That is always interesting and gives us perspective. While many of the details have been lost, we do know something of the specifics of waging a battle on horseback. There are written accounts explaining that horses had to be trained to charge into the chaos of combat and, like the mounted patrols used by city police today, the animals were schooled in ignoring sudden loud noises or other distractions that might naturally cause them to spook or bolt. Training a horse to react coolly under the extreme stresses of combat must have required some extraordinary skill. The animal had to overcome many natural disinclinations to drive into danger rather than flee it. Scrolls left by warriors of the feudal period explain some of the technicalities of *bajutsu,* or horsemanship. We know that stirrups were designed, in part, to be a kind of small battering ram, giving the rider more impact power when kicking in them. Horses were taught to veer off at the last second in a charge against an enemy on foot, giving their rider a chance to make a vicious forward kick. And a few old martial traditions

still teach fighting methods employing the *umahana-neiji*, a device
that controlled the horse and was used to lead it by pinching
the animal's lip, which could also be pressed into service as an
emergency weapon.

This is all interesting from the perspective of the martial arts
historian. But what about the expression under discussion? Because the chances that our karate-do practice will depend upon
our equestrian skills are somewhat small, what has this to do with
our art? Well, admittedly, for the karateka of our day, the expression *buji kore kaere meiba* might have a slightly different connotation than it had either for the feudal warrior or for the modern
Japanese. Consider this:

In our age, the person interested in a fighting art has an almost
incredible array of them from which to choose. Even if we ex-
clude Western combat disciplines such as wrestling and boxing
and just focus on the arts of Asia, the list is amazing. Even if we ex-
clude other Asian fighting arts aside from karate in its Okinawan
and Japanese iterations, in any large city can be found instruction
in more than a dozen flavors. From Shito to Shorin to Shotokan,
from Goju-ryu (available in both Okinawan and Japanese) to
the Kyokushinkai to even smaller, lesser-known systems, the
array is daunting.

So how do you choose? When I began karate-do training in
the 1960s, this was not a problem. Most of us fell into the arts we
practiced because instruction for them was available. If you lived
in Little Rock, Arkansas, for example, you did not say, "Gee, I'd
like to learn the Kobayashi version of the Shorin-ryu," then check
the yellow pages to see where the closest school for that art was.
You took what you could in the way of combat arts—and considered yourself lucky if there was anything at all. As the decades
have gone by, however, and those choices have multiplied, I have
had the opportunity to train in other, different arts. In some cases
I have taken that opportunity. In others, I have passed. Mostly I
have passed because of the constraints of time. My philosophy:
If you do not have time to learn an art well and thoroughly, leave

it alone. I do not want to dabble. In some cases, however, I have deliberately declined taking up an art for another reason. Most of the time that reason is because, while I might find the training interesting and effective, I do not think much of the long-term advantages of following it.

When we are young, we do not think much of these long-term consequences. Our bodies heal quickly; we can ignore minor aches. We are willing to take risks. If driving our fingertips into a tub of sand or gravel will toughen the skin there to allow us to stab through a pine board dramatically, the minor tingle of joint pain in our fingers on cold days is the price we pay. We think little of the cost. The fingers may ache, but they will quickly heal. If full-contact sparring is a way to test the efficacy of our techniques and get the "real-life" reality of fighting, we take it, even though we may also take some punches and kicks to the head in the process—and we take the possibility of concussion or neck injuries along with that. That those injuries could have repercussions in later life seems a distant and hazy possibility. After all, no one lives forever, right?

We are not the first generation, incidentally, to take these risks in return for making ourselves into effective fighters. There are classical martial arts of the feudal age that involve body mechanics that place considerable strain on the knees or other joints. Others involve taking falls onto the hard and unforgiving wooden floor of a dojo. The thought behind this was, "Well, in twenty years I might develop arthritis from this practice. But in twenty days I am going into combat. I am willing to trade the possibility of a future ailment for the increased chances of surviving my next battle." That equation is easy to understand. Warfare in Japan from the middle of the fifteenth century until the beginning of the seventeenth was continual. If you were a fighting man, either a samurai or from another class pressed into military service when the need arose, you had a good chance of seeing combat. So the threat of long-term health problems compared with the realities of looming combat did not usually result in much of a tortuous decision. It is more difficult to understand people today who take a similar approach, who practice as though their personal safety was at immediate risk, and so ignore the possible deleterious consequences of brutal training. The threat of personal combat is not in the immediate future for most of us. We have the luxury of looking at an art dispassionately, considering the long-term ramifications of practicing it. In considering those combat arts—or any physical activity—I consider not just how effective or interesting the art is right now; I think as well what it might do to my body after a couple of decades of training in it. I am not just interested, in other words, in a horse that will carry me into the thick of battle. I want a mount that can carry me through and bring me home safely again.

To be sure, any physical activity has some risk about it. You can develop tendonitis by playing Ping-Pong. And let's be honest: learning to fight is not ever going to be entirely safe. It is the responsibility of every good teacher of a combat art to try to reduce risk wherever reasonable. (Notice I didn't say "wherever *possible*." Big difference. At more advanced levels, it may be possible to reduce risk but it may not be reasonable, not if the goal is to produce an effective fighter.) But it is also the teacher's responsibility to be honest and to explain that antagonistic exercises meant to either simulate or prepare one for combat are, by their nature, sometimes—even often—dangerous. That this is not always explained or followed in practice is a major error in the way Asian combat arts like karate-do have been presented in the West. Where once practitioners made a ridiculously exaggerated show of how "deadly" their training was, now, largely in an attempt to draw in more students and especially children, they have taken an opposite tack. So much is made of the safety factors in the dojo that training is either watered down or entered into without an appropriately sober attitude.

So, when I evaluate a combat art, I am not looking for a risk-free one that might never put me in danger now or as I grow older. I do look, however, for an art in which the benefits are long-term rather than exclusively short-term. Is it healthy to study it now, and will it be when I am in my sixties and beyond? When I see people in their sixties and seventies practicing karate-do, I am often impressed by their technique. I am even more impressed to see them outside the dojo, their stride healthy, their posture good and solid. The way they carry themselves is a testament to their dojo. This is something for you to consider as well, unless you have a plan to be young forever. When you think about what horse it is you want to ride, it might be wise to consider choosing one that can not only get you through the battle, but can bring you home safely.

10

The Front Thrust Kick

The front thrust kick does not get a lot of respect in most dojo. Perhaps it is because there is not a lot of excitement in seeing or performing it. Unlike a front snap kick, that flicks up to head height of an opponent or even higher, cracking like a whip, the forward thrust kick looks more like one is overturning a trash can or stomping at a door that objects to easy opening. The front thrust kick just doesn't have the elegance of the quick, almost ballet-like spring of the snap kick. And unlike that snap kick, it is physiologically impossible to make an effective thrusting kick any higher than you can raise the knee of your kicking leg. Go through the curriculum of your karate kata, and chances are there will not be many sequences that employ the front thrust kick. As a basic tool in the karateka's repertoire, however, this method of kicking can be devastatingly effective. It has a wide range of applications. The front thrust kick should be studied and practiced by anyone who is serious about their training in the art.

The name for the kick in Japanese, *mae-geri kekomi*, or "front kick, thrusting," is accurate. Its derivation is informative. Unlike the *keage,* or "rising kicks," that direct force upward, the energy of a thrust kick goes directly forward—or better yet—*down*. *Age* is from the verb *ageru;* "to rise." *Kekomi* means "to kick in." (You might hear the term *zenpo-giri,* incidentally, which refers collectively to all kicking actions directly in front of the kicker.) Ideally a forward, thrusting kekomi is best used when the target is below the waist of the kicker and when one is doing just that: kicking in. That is primarily because of the way in which the karateka properly prepares for a thrust kick. If you are flexible and have a good springing power in your hips, you can direct the kekomi kick to the chest of an opponent. The problem is that as the leg chambers, with your knee in front of your own chest, your intentions are fairly obvious. If the opponent has even the basic skills of shifting or evading, he is not going to receive the full force of the kick and may be able to avoid it altogether. (Doors don't generally have those talents; that's why a thrusting stomp is so useful in kicking one in.) If you are facing your opponent and his or her knee is cocked up in front of the chest, the ball of the foot pointing in your direction, you don't have to guess to assume what is coming. You can prepare for it, and so defend effectively against it.

In a rising kick, power comes from the upward motion of the foot as well as from its forward momentum. The opponent must deal with energy coming from two directions. In a thrusting kick, the power comes in a single, straight line, directly in. This is another factor in making a kekomi kick that makes it easier to anticipate the kick and to deal with it. The trade-off for the kicker is that the thrusting kick travels with *more* power than does a snap. Again, think about that door. You thrust against it, you do not snap. Traveling in a straight line and backed by the muscles in your hips, the kick may be slower and easier to read by the opponent. If it makes contact, however, it has the potential to do a great deal of damage. There are stories of Okinawan karateka in the eighteenth century who used this kick with such effectiveness against the abdomen of an attacker that the spleen, liver, or other organs were ruptured.

The striking weapon in a front thrust kick is the ball of the foot or the heel. Why not the entire foot? With a hard-soled shoe on, the bottom of the foot might have a strong pushing power. But to strike, to concentrate power in as small an area as possible, you need to focus the contact at those places on the foot most capable of generating that power in a small, focused weapon: the heel or the ball. The heel is harder and less susceptible to injury for the kicker. For it to be the focus of your strike, though, you will need to have considerable flexion in your ankle, drawing back the toes and stretching your calf. Doing the familiar heel-raising exercises with the front of your foot on the edge of a stair riser, or some similar stretching exercise is essential for this kind of flexibility. If your primary weapon in the kick is the ball of the foot, you have to draw the toes back while extending the ball, and your range is limited. Try to kick *in* too high if you are using the ball of the foot and the kick becomes more a snap.

More than any other kick, the mae-geri kekomi depends upon the proper use of the hips. Here is a way to see how this is best done: Stand with your heels together, in a natural stance. Lift your knee and make a thrust kick to the front, at waist height. Now, ask a dojo mate to stand behind you, with his open hand just touching the rear of your head. Kick again and pay attention to what happens to your head. It will move back a couple of inches. If it moves back more, pushing your partner's palm, your power, at least some of it, may be coming from the hips, but it is "leaking" out through your torso. Energy is going backward, not to the target. That's bad.

This next test will look more than a little strange, so do it at home where no one can see you: stand facing a doorway, about six inches from it. Push forward with your hips so your belly touches the doorframe, keeping, as much as possible, your head and shoulders from moving. Yes, I said it looks weird. But you have isolated the muscles in your hips that make a front thrust kick work. The hips must drive forward, giving the kick power and, most important, allowing you great range and distance. The upper body, though, should remain as erect as possible.

Another way of looking at this point is to examine the role of the supporting leg. It cannot be locked. The supporting leg should have some springiness to it, the knee bent just slightly. If you want a guide, have your partner watch you from the side. When your kick connects, your buttocks should be on a vertical plane with the heel of the foot on your supporting leg. The knee of that leg bends just enough to support that action.

Try to keep your hands or fists hanging naturally at your side when you make a front thrust kick. If balance is a problem, you will notice the arms tend to come out to the sides, like a tightrope walker with his balance bar. Avoid that. The less movement you have in your upper body, the more likely this kick will be successful. Which leads us to the front thrust kick's major drawback. No one would describe the mae-geri kekomi as a "stealth" technique. When you are making a front thrust kick, as I noted, it doesn't come as much of a surprise; your knee is chambered, foot cocked—there is not much question where it is going. That means the opponent has only to shift back just enough to let the focus of your kick dissipate in the air in front of him—and you will have basically offered him your leg for grabbing. The front thrust kick is vulnerable to being caught. And the higher its intended target, the more easily it is grabbed. This threat is compounded by the mechanics of the thrust kick. Temporarily, just at contact, a kekomi to the front has the knee locked. If it is intercepted at that instant, your balance is severely compromised to say the least. There are at least two possible solutions to these weaknesses, aside from the oft-heard and good advice that you must retract the kick quickly.

The forward thrust kick is most effective against an attacker's knee or just above the knee. With the kick targeted there, its force tends to come down. It is more like a stomp; the weight of the body and gravity work to add power. If you miss, you will have driven deep into your opponent's stance. Using all caution and good sense, try this exercise to explore the potential of the front thrust kick: Face your partner, both of you in fighting stances. Lift your front knee and make a front kekomi kick aimed either to the inside or outside of his knee. (Let him know in advance which it will be.) Aim deliberately to *miss* the knee and just as important, kick in slow motion, without power. When you miss, instead of retracting your kicking foot, leave it out; drive your body in behind it. In effect, you are making what amounts to a big stomping forward step. You will land well inside the comfort zone of most karateka, in between the legs of his stance. At this point, you should see what sort of close-in techniques are available to you. Again, *use caution.* Your partner is allowing you to come close to his exposed knee with a powerful kick. Don't repay his trust by smashing his kneecap.

The second way of practicing a front thrust kick is one employed by many Okinawan karate systems. Face your partner, both of you in a natural stance. Stand close enough that when you stretch either arm out, you can just pinch his uniform at the shoulder, holding it between your fingertips. This is the distance at which, from time to time, it is illuminating to practice your front thrust kick. Can you lift your knee high enough—moving slowly once again—to be able to connect with your thrust, your foot touching him at waist level, without losing your balance or pulling him? This technique demands a lot of flexibility in the hips. If you have not practiced the basics of the front thrust kick, you will see your weaknesses now come to an unhappy and frustrating fruition. Your buttocks will stick out or you will lean forward, trying to maintain your grip on his sleeve and still get the kick out. In all likelihood, this is the application most often used for the front thrust kick, closer than the distance from which an opponent expects such a kick—or any kick at all. It works well when it is polished, because the opponent fighting close in, even grappling, does not expect a kick and because, properly executed, there isn't any warning. If you and your opponent are at arm's length, his perspective is dramatically shortened. He does not see the knee chambered, he can't anticipate the straightforward direction of the kick.

The mae-geri kekomi will never have the grace and fluid beauty of a front snap kick. Practice it, though, and you will see it definitely has its moments.

11

Better Than Your Sensei

Are you better than your sensei? Do you want to be? Does he or she want you to be?

For most of us, the answer to the first question is an easy one, depending, to some extent, on how we define "better." In most teacher-student relationships, our sensei are older than we are. "Sensei" literally means "the preceding generation." After a certain number of years training, we will be better—if only in terms of our physical condition—than those older than us. Physically, I am stronger than both my sensei, who are getting up in years. I can hit harder, move faster, keep at it longer. In other areas, in matters of timing and distancing and mental control of the dynamics of combat, they are still superior to me. This is one aspect of karate-do and budo in general that separates them from sports or from many other forms of combat. Pure force, energy, strength: all have their place—an important one at that—in any fighting art. Denying that fact is a sentimental conceit, one that puts martial arts all too often in the category of fantasy: the ancient and wizened old master able to send hulking brutes into flight with a flick of the wrist. But perfecting timing, exploiting distancing, and manipulating circumstances during the encounter: these have a significant impact on who goes home at the end of the fight, and they are not dependent upon youth or muscular strength. As one loses muscle mass, strength, and speed, if one is training correctly, one gains in the more subtle aspects of combat. There is no way for a human to avoid losing youth and all the advantages that go with it. If one's practice is solid, however, one can offset those losses considerably by polishing the more subtle particulars of the art. That is not fiction. It is, demonstrably, what allows the older, physically weaker person *through proper training* to defeat those younger and stronger.

That said, it is the remaining two questions that ought to concern all serious students of karate-do. They are by no means easily answered, no matter how we define "better," or in what context. Do you want to be better than your teacher? Does he or she want you to be? You may assume the answers are obvious. They are not. One need only to look at the situation in many, many places where karate is taught to see that.

The image of the sensei in the West has become so ridiculously distorted as to be almost unrecognizable when compared to the original model. And the distortion can be blamed on both students and teachers. On one side are the students, some of them so needy, so eager to have a big daddy or guru who has all the answers, all the power, a person on whom they can rely to unknot any of life's troublesome tangles. Sensei must not only have the most devastating reverse punch possible with the human fist, he must be infinitely wise as well, in matters ranging from advice about marriage or college or vocation to his understanding of the secrets of the universe. On the other side of this image is the teacher himself, too often driven by his own needs for affirmation from those around him, for ego-stroking, for the sense of power he relishes. (In many cases, this flaw is compounded by the sad reality that he is not a teacher at all but rather a person who has exaggerated his own expertise and experience.) This dynamic creates an unhealthy situation. The two reinforce one another. The student needs a leader who is infallible, unbeatable, and infinitely knowledgeable. The teacher needs a sense of superiority to maintain his warped sense of self. Needy people are rarely healthy people, psychologically speaking. Putting them together, one feeding off the other, is not a recipe for a mature relationship in the dojo or anywhere else.

In the reality of a healthy teacher-student relationship of the kind fostered in a good karate dojo, the sensei must be like a parent, one with a healthy and realistic sense of who he is, who his children are, and what he wishes them to become. Little is more pathetic than the father who still tries to compete with his teenage boy in physical challenges, or the mother who wants to be viewed in the same way as her daughter in terms of youth and beauty. Good parents not only accept that they will be surpassed by their children in many areas, they welcome it. The idea that their child will get a better education, a better career, will see and do more in life than they have—these potentials and possibilities excite the parent. The healthy parent does not view the success of his or her child as a threat but rather as a testament to his or her good parenting.

No analogy is perfect: I don't entirely like comparing a sensei and his adult students to a parent and child. But in some ways, it reflects the relationship. When someone walks into your dojo the first time, no matter what his age, he is like a child in terms of his understanding and capacity for learning. As a teacher, you have to lead him. What happens, though, when he matures, just like a child does in a family? When he has graduated and is ready to pursue a career? Does the parent continue to lead him, making decisions for that child? We don't "graduate" from the martial arts. There is always more to learn. One of my sensei continued to train with his teacher until that teacher died, long after my sensei had been given a full, formal license of mastery in the art. Another sensei of mine continues to train with his teacher even though he, too, has been given by that teacher a full license. The relationship between teacher and student, though, evolved over time. They disagree on things, on how techniques or kata should be taught, what should be emphasized, how far in this direction or that a student should be allowed to stray from the model the teacher sets. The teacher and his student, who has in his own right become a teacher as well, are more like equals. One will always bow a little lower, of course, and use the more polite forms of speech in Japanese. Still, the teacher has recognized his pupil has matured and must be allowed to go his own way. That does not mean splitting from the teacher; it means carrying out his teaching to the best of one's ability—even if that results in some conflict or disagreement from time to time.

The point here is that the teacher wishes and expects his student to exceed him. The teacher does not need to have all the answers, to be the final authority, to control everything that goes on in the student's life. A good parent does not need to tell you, as an adult, which job to take, who to marry, or where to live in order to feel good about himself. He does not have to control every part of your life. He has given you the skills to do that yourself; now he's proud and rewarded to see you do just that.

There are some martial arts teachers—way too many—who do not take the mature parent approach. The idea that a student might exceed them in talent is frightening and threatening. A student might eventually be given teaching authority by one of these teachers, but every aspect of the curriculum, every exercise and training method, will have to undergo the scrutiny of the teacher. The student in effect never becomes a sensei himself, and is never elevated in the estimation of others to the same position as his teacher. His teacher will always remind him of his "place."

These teachers resort to all sorts of schemes and ploys to maintain their status. Most are ridiculous, propped up with vague explanations of how "this is the way it's done in Japan" and such. Some are actually absurd. Even in Japan, these efforts at maintaining status among those in charge are unfortunately common. One major Japanese karate organization has it as an official policy

that no non-Japanese will ever be given a black belt *dan* grade
higher than fifth dan. This is laughable, of course, and grossly rac-
ist. It is obviously meant to keep the Japanese on a pedestal. They
surely could not stay up there by technique and skill, since some
of their Western students have long ago surpassed them in these
areas. Nobody is supposed to notice that, however, and the silly
"rank by race" rule is meant to draw a curtain over that potentially
embarrassing fact.

Equally silly are the tricks teachers play to keep up the façade
in the dojo. A teacher will tell students his techniques are so advanced and deadly now that he cannot really get on the floor
and perspire and train with his students because it would be too
dangerous for the students. (Let me be clear: if you have trained
more than ten years and have not practiced with your teacher as
an equal, sparred, or gone through kata as attacker and defender,
back and forth, you and he are not doing a serious martial art.)
Other teachers use outlandish ranking to try to maintain their superiority. "Well yes, I'm a Supreme Grand Master. But my teacher
is an *Ultimate* Supreme Grand Master." Is this a karate organization or a fantasy cartoon?

You should have every desire and expectation to surpass your
teacher. While this may seem obvious, for many people involved
in karate-do or other budo, there is a real fear of doing just that.
These students' egos require reinforcement in a different way
than does that of the needy teacher. This reinforcement, however,
is no less damaging. To surpass my teacher means that my teacher
is not the omnipotent force I feel I need. If my technique is better than his, that means his is not perfect. And so in what other
ways might my teacher also be less than perfect? It is frightening
for these students to contemplate that possibility. Sensei doesn't
have all the answers? Sensei isn't the model of perfection itself?
Then what does it say about me that I am following him?

To recognize that your teacher has limitations is not to suggest
he is not worth emulating or that he is not or should not be the
source of your karate-do instruction. To realize that if you train

hard you will eventually be as good as he is—or possibly even better—does not mean you won't always respect and cherish him or her. Similarly, you should have the same desires and expectations to do better than your parents. That is what they reared you to do. Surpassing my teacher does not mean he is no longer my teacher. It rather means I have honored him by going further into the art, something I'd never have been able to do without his guidance. As important, as a teacher, you need to always expect your students to surpass you. Whether they do or not, your students are, in the end, the only evidence we will ever have that you were a "sensei" in the first place.

12

What's in a Name?

Every once in a while it is worthwhile to go back to the basics...

We use the term "martial arts" all the time when talking about karate. We take both the term and the description of karate as a martial art to be obvious. In recent years, "mixed martial arts" has become a common way to describe competition that pits exponents of many different combat arts in a ring to see who can win according to the rules of the organization sponsoring the event. "Martial arts" has become such a universally understood expression we take its meaning for granted. At times, it is worthwhile to reexamine this. What exactly is a martial art? Most of us would answer that question with "karate" or "kung fu" or we might mention many of the other well-known combat systems practiced today. The martial arts are "arts for fighting," we would say, and that seems fairly straightforward. OK. However, we have to be careful if we define a martial art as synonymous with a fighting art. Is, for example, boxing a martial art? How about pistol shooting? Archery?

To begin, we must acknowledge that this matter of nomenclature is a tricky one and there are no hard and fast rules. The word "martial" is one, of course, with a Latin origin, along with some contributions from the Greek. It was the Greeks who deified Ares as a god of war; later he became known to the Romans as Mars. It is a safe bet that few of the warrior class of old Japan who created and used these fighting arts we are talking about was conversant in Latin. Or Greek. So we are borrowing words from our own culture to describe something in another culture, in this case, Japan's. That can make the semantics even more complicated, murkier. If you don't think so, consider this: Ares or Mars is not actually the Olympian god of war, though such an answer would be acceptable in the average trivia game. In Greek, a distinction is made between normal warfare and the sort of bloodlust savagery that sometimes erupted on the battlefield. Ares personified this particular kind of warfare; in English we do not have a convenient equivalent that separates the two, and neither did the Romans. So when Ares became Mars, there was already a borrowing that led to a loss of precise definition. It was further mutated by our own English definition of "war."

The closest approximation in Japanese to "martial" is the word *bu*. Most readers probably know this. They would recognize *bu* as a prefix in budo (martial Ways), bushido (the Way of the bushi, or warrior), and so on. It would be a mistake, though, to assume that *bu* has exactly the same connotations and definition in Japanese culture as the word "martial" does in ours.

In Japan, since early times, the role of the warrior was much more fixed than in the West. There were, it is true, many periods in Japanese history in which nonprofessional men, farmers or merchants or whatever, were pressed into military service. They were similar to the "citizen-soldiers" that we have had in our Minutemen and militias (except for the important distinction that they usually did not have the freedom to choose to fight or not). But by the fourteenth century, when feudalism had become a fixture of social and political life in Japan, the status of the warrior was more or less relegated to members of a specific, hereditary caste. You will notice that I am using all kinds of qualifying language here, "more or less," and that sort of thing. There were exceptions—important ones, like the case of Hideyoshi Toyotomi, who rose from the status of a commoner to that of Japan's most powerful ruler during his lifetime. It is also important to observe that just because the samurai were a fixture in the caste system did not mean they lacked other jobs and responsibilities. Samurai spent more time as accountants, civil engineers, and tax collectors than they did on the battlefield. That said, the farmer who took up a sword or a spear and went out and fought for his clan or his daimyo was the oddity in the history of warfare in Japan from the fourteenth century on. Battlefield fighting was a job for professional fighters: the samurai.

The samurai evolved their own behaviors, their own ways of approaching conflict, and their own arts. Swordsmanship, for instance, was a method of fighting that would have had limited use or interest for the non-warrior. Learning to fortify a position was an art that few farmers would have had need for. These were martial arts in the sense that they were the exclusive domain of the professional martial artist. In Japanese, these arts were called the *bugei* or the *bujutsu*, the "martial crafts" or "martial arts." There are, to further sharpen this point, many martial arts from old Japan that are not fighting arts. The art of effectively signaling troops during massed movements, for example, was an involved and complex one. Commanders had to be skilled in composing brief but critical orders. These in turn had to be passed on, via flags or smoke signals or through mediums such as conch-shell trumpets that could be sounded in different ways to get across the message. These arts were essential to the warrior, even though they did not directly involve actual combat.

In other countries in Asia, there were different histories and different developments. In China, for example, there was never a clearly delineated warrior class. There are some weapons there that were of use primarily on the battlefield, and the arts devoted to these weapons might properly be called martial arts. For the most part, however, kung fu and other combat arts of China are, from a semantic perspective, just that: combat arts. Fighting arts. But not martial arts. Remember: we are not talking about the *effectiveness* of an art. The observation that this or that fighting art is not really a martial art often elicits anger in practitioners of those arts, and they are quick to protest. "Don't think my *wing chun* kung fu is a martial art, eh? How about we go out on the floor and I show you just how martial it can be?" The exception taken is misplaced. There are remarkably efficient fighting arts and methods out there. We are not talking, in this context, about how good or practical an art may be in the sense of combat. We are looking at the history and aims of the art. If it was used on the battlefield, by professional men-at-arms, it is, properly speaking, a martial art. If it wasn't, it isn't.

In the same way, as you may have guessed, karate would not be considered a martial art. A professional fighting class never used it. There is some evidence—and it is far from conclusive—that karate owes much of its original development to a gentrified group of scholars, aristocrats, law-enforcement officers, royal guards, and others of an upper and gentrified class. This group, known collectively as *pechin*, no doubt had an impact on karate. They are sometimes referred to as the Okinawan equivalent of the samurai. The comparison is not entirely exact. Okinawa did not have a standing army; its inhabitants did not engage in internecine warfare or in war against other countries. There was little opportunity for the pechin class to develop combat skills with a truly martial component to them. Karate, nevertheless, could in some light be considered an Okinawan martial art. But it is stretching things a bit to consider the pechin a professional fighting class of men. Karate was essentially an art of the nonprofessional warrior. Certainly there was not a single Okinawan karateman who could be considered a full-time fighter from a historical perspective—or even, as with the samurai, a person exclusively identified by his martial status. Nor would they have wanted to be, I don't think. Instead, karate was a civilian combat art. It remains so today.

Most readers will know that the traditional fighting arts of the samurai, some of them anyway, still exist today. Commonly, we refer to these arts as the bujutsu or the bugei, or they are referred to as the *koryu*, the "old schools." They live on for various reasons: as a part of cultural identification, as "living antiques" that offer unique perspectives on Japan's past, or for the psychological insights they offer into conflict. Needless to say, no one studies one of these arts for use on the battlefield. Still, they are "martial" in the true sense of that word.

So, we have made a broad distinction between martial arts and fighting arts. Not all martial arts, as we have noted, are directly applicable as fighting arts. And sometimes, too, the definition blurs. There are combat arts, such as pistol shooting, that could be classified as either martial or fighting. The shooting done by law-enforcement personnel or that which is taught as a means of self-defense for civilians is not a martial art. But the marksmanship with a pistol that is taught in the military could be. This distinction works in the opposite direction. *Jukendo,* for example, is the art of killing with a bayonet mounted on a rifle, a system that was developed by the military in Japan, mostly inspired by bayonet fighting the Japanese observed in European armies during the first part of the twentieth century. It was developed in modern times, but it would, according to our definition, be a martial art. Many of its advocates today, however, like to think of jukendo as a *do,* a martially-inspired Way in which the martial aspects of the art are superseded by its physical, moral, and aesthetic values.

This is, as we should see by now, a difficult concept to explain and understand. We like to have clear-cut definitions: "this art belongs in that category, that art belongs in this one." Unfortunately for those of us who like these neat definitions, the Japanese language is not particularly accommodating. It has become popular and convenient for scholars to distinguish between martial Ways (budo) and martial arts (bujutsu or bugei). Martial arts are the older, battlefield forms. Judo, karate-do, and aikido are examples of martial Ways. The problem with this is that there were many feudal-era martial arts which, in their own texts, refer to themselves as budo forms. And there are modern arts, such as jukendo, that like to call themselves bujutsu, even though they were developed decades after the end of the samurai.

It does not matter so much what terms we use, I suppose. We who practice karate-do can continue to call ourselves martial artists. It is important, though, for us to understand the meanings behind these words and to know that what is in the name of an art can be the first step in learning what that art is all about.

13

You Have to Hit Stuff

We have all heard the words of the cynic who, upon seeing a demonstration of karate's *tameshiwari,* or breaking techniques, sneers that "boards don't hit back." The tone is snide. The intent is dismissive, a reference to the relative value (or lack thereof) for the karateka in the practice of breaking boards or bricks or other inanimate objects. Literally, *tameshiwari* means "a test of breaking": *tameshi* is "to experiment" or "test," while *wari* means "to split" or "sunder." Tameshiwari has become, along with the pajama-clad exponent and frenzied yelling, one of the classic clichés of karate-do. Shattering knee-high stacks of lumber is the quintessential image many people have of karate training. Some karate-do purists dismiss it all as showboating, an embarrassing spectacle that threatens to reduce karate-do to the status of a sideshow stunt. And those sneering critics scoff, noting that since those boards or bricks or ceramic roofing tiles do not pose much of a threat, the conditions for breaking are inevitably controlled, and so what is the point? It is a lot easier to wind up and whack a stack of pine than it is to strike an opponent who is moving and, further, is intent on hitting you. The criticisms have some validity. True, boards and bricks don't strike back the same way a live, animated opponent might. Unfortunately, as most of those who have done it at least a few times have learned through the bitter lessons of sprained wrists, broken knuckles, and some impressive bruises, boards and the like indeed *do* hit back sometimes.

The ability of lumber or other inanimate objects to attack aside, striking various forms of building materials may have a limited usefulness in practicing and polishing one's karate-do. Mostly it is for show, of course, as is so often alleged. That is not to say that hitting things is bad, however. Karate is a percussive art. The thought that one can become good at it without actually "percussing" something is fanciful. Fanciful, but distressingly common among too many karateka. Far too much time is spent in many karate dojo punching and kicking against nothing more substantial than air. The emphasis on that sort of training leads to an unrealistic appreciation of what it is like to encounter resistance to one's attacks. To believe you can attain competency in a striking art without actually ever hitting anything is unlikely to lead to a balanced understanding of one's abilities.

Boxing, of course, makes extensive use of striking objects: heavy bags and speed bags are always to be found in boxing gyms. As for Japanese arts that feature striking, making physical contact with similar equipment is by no means a modern innovation. In many classical schools of combat from the feudal era, some of which still survive, a fundamental part of training involves using a wooden sword or even just a club or stick to strike a target with full force and power. In the Jigen-ryu, a powerful school of swordsmanship from southern Japan, near-daily use is made of a vertical striking post that consists of a tree trunk about the diameter of a basketball goalpost. The exponent uses a wooden sword and unleashes a series of attacks, striking again and again, uttering a piercing shriek that is the distinctive *kiai* of the school. These posts, in use in Jigen-ryu dojo for generations, are worn down from countless strikes and often have deep grooves, looking like someone has carved pieces out of them. This kind of training is epitomized by an adage from the ryu that "the dragonfly always returns to the post." What it means, among other things, is that a committed swordsman will drive his way to his target no matter what comes up to prevent him, much like a dragonfly that will land on a post or weed stalk, buzzing away but always coming back to the same place.

Other classical ryu use the trunk of a living tree for such training, or a device that looks like a pair of sawhorses with a bundle of thick branches laid between them that can be struck vertically. With the advent of rubber tires, martial arts schools in the early twentieth century saw an even better way to engage in "full contact" training with equipment. They mounted a motorcycle tire on a rack or tied it against a tree that could be used for striking. The resistance provided by the rubber is an excellent way to develop hitting power.

In karate, of course, the makiwara has long been the favored training tool for striking. Accurately described as looking like a parking meter, it is a wooden post, either fixed to the floor or sunk into the ground. Traditionally, it is topped with a sheaf of woven rice straw, or more likely today, a pad of rubber or other material designed to give a bit, usually encased in a cloth or vinyl sheath. The origins of the makiwara are obscure. Some Chinese arts use striking posts, like wing chun's wooden dummy, which features peglike appendages useful for practicing the skills of grabbing or blocking. The makiwara may have been an adaptation of this training tool or something like it, imported from China. But many Chinese combat arts, particularly the internal ones, like tai chi and *hsing i,* downplay or actually forbid this kind of supplemental training equipment. One reason is a belief, held by some Chinese practitioners and possibly based on traditional Chinese health systems, that hitting hard objects repeatedly can have an adverse effect on the eyes. So goes the theory: the repeated jarring of the head that comes from hitting an object over and over again sets up an unhealthy kind of vibration that is injurious to the delicate muscles of the eye. There is no doubt the makiwara can be misused. Karateka who bashed away at it until their knuckles bled, the skin torn to the bone, were a familiar sight in Japan before and immediately after the war. The macho image of big, deformed knuckles covered in calluses was and is appealing to a lot of young men wanting to look tough. The crippling, disfiguring arthritis and other bone ailments that often follow them into middle age aren't so impressive. Nearly all striking arts, though, include hitting devices such as boxing's heavy bag—implements that will give when hit yet are solid enough to provide some realistic resistance. Striking dummies made of various plastics that have the look and feel of a human body have become popular and, while expensive, they are excellent for hitting. It is fair to say one can learn a lot by connecting a punch to one of these objects. Beginner karateka are often astonished at how easily their wrists collapse with the first strike.

A word here about repeatedly hitting stones or anvils or other solid objects: don't. I know a lot of Japanese and Okinawan karate practitioners do it. It looks cool. There is no evidence that it will do anything for you, just as big calluses are not evidence of a greater striking ability. Consider: when you hit something, something must give. It will either be the striking weapon or the target. No matter how strong you are, you are not denser than a stone or a brick wall or a chunk of steel. The force of the strike is going back into your hand. Confine your hitting to stuff that will give at least a little.

It is easy to go overboard once you incorporate striking into your training and workouts. There is a satisfaction in hitting something full force, seeing the makiwara rock or the heavy bag sway or bend or kink. The beginner, in particular, is tempted to whack away until he can no longer lift his arms. Next morning, he will feel a lot of stiffness in his joints. When he is young, in most cases the stiffness will work itself out in a few days. It is easy, though, to do some real damage, no matter what one's age. Sometimes the effect is cumulative. Sometimes it does not become clinical and noticeable until years later. While you may feel indestructible, take it easy. Becoming comfortable with hitting stuff that has resistance takes time. Muscle, sinew, and bone have to become accustomed to the shock. In the case of the makiwara, particular care must be taken. Karateka in old Okinawa knew how to build one, how to pad it, and how to use it. (Some of this was arcane and questionable from a practical view. It was tradition, for instance, that a makiwara be put into the ground by moonlight. In other cases, though, applications of local herbs and other potions kept infections and swelling to a minimum, and practitioners were learning under teachers who knew how to apply such medications.) This knowledge is not so prevalent today. So be patient. And do not be afraid to back off if the stiffness of the pad seems excessive. A makiwara should flex a little; the pad should absorb some of the shock. Put the heel of your hand, arm outstretched, against the makiwara pad. Give a push. If the makiwara doesn't move or give at least an inch, it is too stiff. It must be modified, usually by shaving down some of the thickness in the post.

The heavy bag is easier to hit than a makiwara—though wrist injuries are still common. The bag offers another advantage in that, in swaying with your strikes, you get some feel of hitting a moving target. It is possible to incorporate body shifting and evading and other movements into your striking workout with a heavy bag. One good exercise—boxers or karateka who use a bag regularly will know many others, and it is worthwhile to watch them in the gym or dojo—is to hit the bag to start it moving, then keep hitting it so it never comes back to hang perfectly straight. How long can you keep it from swinging back to the upright, vertical position? Striking the heavy bag this way combines an aerobic workout with your hitting practice. A heavy bag is also an important piece of equipment in teaching karateka the danger of locking out their elbows as they punch. Beginners tend to do this, sometimes carrying the habit along as they progress. Lock your elbow in a punch against the heavy bag and it will definitely "hit" back, the weight of the bag driving back all the way to your shoulder in an unpleasant shock.

So how much of your training should be given to this sort of striking practice? If you train for two hours in a regular class or on your own, probably forty minutes of that time should be devoted to hitting something. This may surprise "traditionalists" who spend relatively little time, if any, on the makiwara or heavy bag. But hitting something that hits back in the form of resistance is valuable in developing technique. It will improve your karate considerably.

14

What Does a Black Belt Mean?

The black belt is—or has become—far more than just a symbol of rank in the karate dojo and to the public at large. It has an aura about it. It has a connotation. What is the first thing the average person thinks of when you say "black belt" in reference to karate-do or martial arts in general? Masterful skill. Extraordinary abilities. The black belt is the mark of an expert. Those actually training in a particular art might have a more objective, less sensationalized definition. If you have been pursuing karate-do for any time at all, long enough in particular to have attained a rank symbolized by that belt, you will have a more nuanced perception, probably. You will understand a great deal about what has gone into reaching that level. If you are fortunate, you will understand much more about what lies beyond that level. Nevertheless, we have to admit that the popular image of the black belt is inextricably woven into the general perception of these arts we follow. While we may have a more comprehensive view of the belt, we need to see that in the population outside the dojo, in the world at large, it usually means something else. When a black belt is conferred upon a karateka, that has implications in the popular imagination. And we should consider some ramifications that perception and those implications in turn have upon what people think about karate-do.

Most readers will know that the belt system (dan-i) was created entirely by judo's founder, Jigoro Kano. It has no ancient, feudal, or samurai connections. Belts in black or any other color were not a part of martial arts practice before the twilight of the feudal period in Japan, which ended in 1867. Kano awarded the first black belts around the turn of the last century. Karate-do and other Japanese arts adopted the system, and later on so did most Korean combat arts.

The Japanese martial arts that existed previously in that country's history, those going back to the feudal period, had an entirely different way of giving rank within their curriculum. The *menkyo* system is one still employed by many traditional arts of Japan, including flower arranging and tea ceremony. Nearly all classical martial arts of the feudal period used some variation of this system, and those extant today continue to use it. A series of licenses and sometimes accompanying scrolls were given to the student at various periods in the education. In some cases the menkyo verified that the student had reached a particular level of understanding. In many instances, these documents symbolized an official license to teach or otherwise represent the school. Often the wording in these menkyo scrolls was flowery and elaborate: "Having been revealed by the deities, this extraordinary skill, known far and wide across the land, is hereby transmitted to the recipient of this document . . ." That's the typical tone of a menkyo. When one cuts through all that florid hyperbole, however, the overall message is usually clear. The recipient of the scroll or paper is officially recognized in some capacity by the headmaster of that school. It is relatively easy to determine what this capacity is in the wording of the document. That is a significant difference in these older arts and in the more modern combat arts like karate-do, which award ranks. Correspondingly, what exactly the black belt signifies in the modern dojo is another question entirely.

When the typical student begins training, he is apt to think the black belt means the wearer has arrived at a high level of competence. In some dojo perhaps this is true. In most organized modern budo such as karate, however, a black belt is generally given after a few years of training. Looking through the rank qualifications of several Japanese karate-do organizations, I found four years to be about the average time required to reach *shodan,* or a first level black belt, assuming one trains and tests regularly within that organization. In many of these schools, the black belt is a signal you are considered a student committed to your study and you are now ready to begin training in earnest. In other words, the black belt is a sign you have walked through the door and little else. You are not an expert. Not a teacher. Certainly not a master. You are not even someone who can adequately represent the art. The belt means you have stuck it out long enough to warrant some serious consideration as a student, period.

In Japan, it is not uncommon to see sixteen- or seventeen-year-old children with black belts. By that time the young people have been in the dojo or training in their school's budo clubs for probably close to ten years. No one in Japan would regard them as anything like a "master," of course, just because they were wearing a black belt. The budo are a part of that country's culture, so while it would be absurd to suggest the average Japanese knows anything about budo in any specialized way, they do know enough not to hold a black belt wearer in the kind of awe people sometimes do in the West. (In fact, most Japanese I have known understand that karate is about kicking and judo is about throwing, and that's pretty much the extent of their grasp of the subtleties of budo.)

It would be nice if we had a similar understanding of what a black belt means here, but we do not. We have evolved some different perspectives in the roughly half-century that budo has been widely practiced in the United States, some of them fairly strange. I can remember back in the 1960s when some people seriously believed that in order to get a black belt, you had to kill a person. Or that you had to openhandedly chop through a requisite number of boards successfully. The general public has become a little more sophisticated now, but that's not to say they don't still have some odd ideas. The status of the black belt is among them.

This morning's paper contains a story about a "black belt" in a local karate school. He has been training for about two years and has competed successfully in several tournaments. He was recently promoted to a black belt rank. He is nine years old.

How do you react to a nine-year-old with a black belt? On one hand, I can look at it from a Japanese perspective (though even in Japan this would be a bit young). The kid's been training hard regularly and the teacher is giving him a rank that reflects that.

I tend to look at it, though, from a Western perspective. And from that side of things, there is nothing good that comes from awarding a black belt to a child. Here's why: As we have discussed, for better or worse, the perception of a black belt is different here than in Japan. The public sees a child with a black belt and they assume that, in this dojo at least, training is literally kid's stuff. They expect some level of competence and skill in a black belt that they know no child that age has or could have. How well would that nine-year-old do against a twenty-one-year-old black belt in competition, they would ask. Since karate is inextricably linked with personal defense, they wonder too how the kid would do against a serious threat by an adult attacker. And while you could try to explain that this is a special junior rank or that a black belt does not necessarily signify an objective level of technical competence in all holders, it all sounds like rationalization to the public. You are giving the kid a black belt either because you want to encourage more children to enroll and thus pay the bills, or because it has to do with some other profit-motivated scheme,

or because you just do not take your art seriously. That is going
to be the assumption. Come on. If a child can get a black belt in
your art, how much is a black belt worth? Or for that matter, how
much can your art itself be worth?

Awarding a black belt to a preadolescent smacks of the kind
of grade inflation we have all heard so much about in education.
Students are being awarded A's merely for showing up to class
regularly. High school students graduate without being able to
competently read the words on this page—and I am not talking about the words in Japanese. As a result, straight A's or a high
school diploma no longer have the value or meaning they once
did. The same can be said about a black belt. And certainly the
argument can be made that if the black belt does not convey the
aura of mastery or great, almost magical, expertise it once did,
that's really a step in the right direction. Nonetheless, I think martial arts schools should do a lot of thinking before making promotions of this type.

Unless we are training in that school, it is impossible for us to
make a complete judgment on the quality of skill necessary to
obtain a black belt. So we do not know if the child in question
deserves such a rank or not. That's not what I'm talking about.
What I am suggesting is that the perception of the public, when
they see a kid walking around in a dojo wearing a black belt, has
some considerable resonances in how the public will view your
art and your school. Indeed, I am told that some schools are having trouble attracting adolescents or young adults for that very
reason. These are the age groups who have the maturity, the
physical abilities, and the income to make training in a martial art
a long-term investment of time and energy. They are the group
that will stick around long enough to keep the dojo solvent and
healthy. If they are turned away by the sight of a black belt not
that many years out of diapers, that does not portend well for the
future of the school.

Sure, it is great publicity. A black belt promotion—"and he's
only nine years old!"—is the stuff of local news stories. And it

may attract other kids. You can argue further that having a big children's class is your way to pay the bills, to make it possible for the dojo to operate so that older, more serious students will have a place to train. You might want to look around though, and see if your means—giving black belts to children—is actually producing the ends you say you want: a mature dojo where mature people are coming to follow a serious Way.

15

Victory Is in the Scabbard

Saya no uchi de katsu. "Victory is in the scabbard" is a rough translation of this bit of advice that comes from the era in Japan when
swords were worn daily and put to their intended use on a not-
infrequent basis. A less poetic way of translating it would be that
victory—*katsu*—is determined by the potential of the sword
before it is drawn, while it is still resting in the *saya,* or scabbard. If
you are a karateka, even if you have never handled a sword at all,
this maxim and its implications are worth your consideration.

First, there is an enormous difference between a violent conflict in which one or both sides are unarmed, and a fight where
one or both participants have weapons. Many karate practitioners who spend their time in the study of unarmed combat
do not appreciate fully the extreme advantage one has in fighting when armed with even a simple weapon. Give one person a
roll of quarters around which to wrap the fist and that person is
much, much more dangerous than an opponent who is punching or hitting with only the hands. A stick in one's grasp—any
stick, from the size of a pencil on up to the size and dimensions

of an oar—affords opportunities and advantages that can make a person far more effective in a fight. When the weapon becomes a firearm, most of us can see this difference more clearly. Only in movies does a protagonist effortlessly disarm a gun-wielding bad guy. This, of course, is why self-defense courses so often stress the importance of looking around in a confrontation or attack to see if there is anything that can be used as a weapon. It is why, while they may have an élan about them, unarmed fighting systems almost always are for sport or ritual, or they are the product of a people who have been denied weapons for one reason or another.

In the spectrum between unarmed and being maximally armed (a gun would probably define the latter in terms of personal combat), a sword is somewhere in between in our estimation of the threat posed by weapons. It is more dangerous, we understand, than a stick or blunt object. But the sword is not as lethal, we know, as a firearm, which can kill at a distance. Frankly, that is about all most karateka—and people in general—know about the sword. This relative unfamiliarity with a bladed weapon makes it difficult for us to place in proper context sayings and epigrams such as the one we are discussing here. Swords just have not played a big role in our history as Americans. They are more in the realm of ancient history or fantasy for us. To get a better perspective, we have to put ourselves in the historical position of the samurai. If you were a member of that class, in many periods throughout the history of feudal Japan you were constantly armed. The sword was a part of your everyday wear. And everyone else in your caste was carrying one as well. In addition, many non-samurai who were legally allowed to carry swords were also armed. (During much of their time at the top of Japan's caste system, the samurai were not distinguished by their swords. It was rather their privilege to carry both a long and short sword together that separated them from other castes.) Imagine spending much of your day being surrounded by colleagues who are all openly carrying pistols in holsters, as well as by others in your neighborhood—mail carriers, shop clerks, doctors—going about their businesses similarly armed. Someone has said that a well-armed society is a polite society. That may be so. Unquestionably, when one has a sword or other such weapon at one's side that is so easily able to be used to kill or cripple, one is apt to incline toward one of two personalities. Either he develops the manner of a barbarian tyrant, or he becomes a sober man who lives with the knowledge that *any* actions with that weapon will have definitive consequences.

If I am attacking you or being threatening, and you deliver a reverse punch to my head, you may cause some damage: a black eye, a broken jaw, a loosened tooth. Only in extreme situations, though, will your punch result in my being permanently crippled or dead. It happens, but not often. And you are, in most cases, not thinking of killing or crippling me when you punch. You wish only to address the attack or threat and nullify it. In the same situation, however, were you carrying a sword and you drew it, chances are infinitely greater that irreparable harm or death would come my way. Or, if I am also carrying a sword and we have a conflict, you will draw yours with the understanding that you may also be crippled or killed.

My point here is that for the samurai, it was not just having a sword that distinguished him from other social classes. It was the constant awareness of the *potential* of the sword. Its consequences, in use, were severe. They were stark; black and white. Live or die. (Some familiar with the mechanics of Japanese swordsmanship and Japan's history will note I am being overly dramatic. Swords could wound. Not every violent encounter with them ended in death. That is a historical fact. However, remember that we are talking about the potential of the sword. Even a minor wound with the sword could inflict grievous damage that might not have killed outright but which could have led to infection or other crippling injuries that would have eventually led to death. The point is not that the sword killed each time it was drawn, but that death was a real threat whenever a sword was employed.)

Certainly law-enforcement personnel and the military live with this reality as well. They are armed, if not constantly, at least in the normal course of their day. They carry weapons that can kill. They have a legal right to use them, often in a rather broad scope of circumstances. Ask anyone acquainted with violence, however, and they will tell you, as I mentioned earlier, that there is a big difference between shooting someone, even from a close distance, and the intimacy required in cutting someone with a knife or sword. It is more personal and more daunting in some ways. There is an immediacy to the act. This immediacy is implied in the various names used in Japanese to describe drawing the sword. The *iai* of *iaido* or *iaijutsu*—terms used for the formal exercises of drawing and cutting—means "to take initiative" or "to seize the moment." *Iai* implies a conclusive action. *Batto*, another such term, means "the sword that hits instantly." *Nuki uchi*, the expression used in the maxim we are discussing, is "to strike while emptying the scabbard." Given the nature of the Japanese sword and the ways it is most effectively used, there is a single moment—a single movement—that defines the outcome.

On one hand, we can interpret that "victory is determined in the scabbard" in a "let's live in harmony and use our martial arts to promote world peace, and so the sword that's left in the scabbard is the one that really signifies mastery of our art" kind of altruism. On one level, this is what the saying can imply. On another, though, the idea that winning the victory begins with the sword still sheathed has more profound implications.

We in the karate dojo are at the opposite end of this spectrum of potential lethality. Our concerns are with using our bodies effectively in fighting, and no matter how well trained, even the world's best karateka cannot do as much damage as swiftly to another human as even an untrained person with a sword. That acknowledged, the potential for damage, for a violent confrontation, is always within us. The "my body is a weapon" stuff is the cheesy nonsense of bad novels and worse movies. Nevertheless, if the skills are there, if you have internalized your art, refined your responses, polished your abilities, then the potential is still there. In the beginner, it will not be so serious. In the expert, it will be considerable. How do you deal with that? Do you become cocky, careless in paying attention to the sorts of situations that can lead to conflict? Or do you go the opposite direction, concerned about and mindful of the violence that is within you?

If you were able to carry a firearm or a sword with you at all times, to be constantly armed, would you feel safer? Or would you become paranoid, seeing threats in every dark corner? Or, modify the question: would you feel safer or more threatened if everyone went about armed? This is not an argument for or against gun control. Or one devoted to the advisability of carrying a weapon as a consistent means of self-defense. For the samurai, being armed was a given. He had the power, both in terms of his weapon and his status, to kill. It was always right there beside him, day and night. It is romantic silliness to say that the best samurai was the one who always avoided a fight. He was a professional warrior. He sometimes *had* to fight. True, he was most effective when he or his leader could devise a strategy that gained victory without drawing the sword. That said, once the need arose, he could not hesitate in drawing the weapon.

I think one meaning of "victory is in the scabbard" is in the acceptance of one's powers and skills. I think it also signifies that one has considered fully and carefully the consequences of using them. It would be nice if we could map out every possible scenario where confrontation might occur: "OK, I'll fight in this situation, but I won't in that one." Life, we know, is not like that. Situational ethics is a philosophy only for the simple-minded. We have to have basic principles, basic ideas of right and wrong. Yet human interaction is so varied, with so many shades of gray, that we cannot possibly foresee every conflict and decide ahead of time how we will meet it. The consequences of how we do meet it, though, are, as I noted above, starkly black and white in retrospect. The swordsman had a choice: pull his weapon from its sheath or leave it. Even if our karate is not so lethal in most situations, we have the same choice. We fight because we can. We have the talent for it. We do not fight for exactly those same reasons as did the samurai. We are not so different from those who constantly carried a sword and felt its weight. We should feel the weight as well, and be constantly cognizant of all its implications.

16

Kyan Chotoku's Legacy

One legendary story about Kyan Chotoku was that he confronted a bully named Matsuda when the latter was being particularly obnoxious. Because Kyan Chotoku (1870–1945) was so diminutive, even by Okinawan standards, Matsuda thought he would have no problem in a fight. Not only was the diminutive Kyan so much smaller than Matsuda, Kyan had, unfortunately and unwisely it appeared, situated himself on the bank of the Hija River on Okinawa, with no place to run. The Hija empties out into the Pacific right beside the city of Kadena, now best known as the site of a massive U.S. military installation. The bridge on which Kyan and Matsuda met is a long one, made of stones, with five separate spans connected. It was as far upriver as trading ships could travel back in the late nineteenth century, when the spans were built, so the neighborhood was congested with shops and traffic. (Miraculously, it survived the bombing of World War II.)

Anyway, back to the action. Why the men were fighting, no one knows. One account suggests Matsuda was a local bully and was challenged by Kyan. Whatever the cause, the fight was on,

Matsuda was charging, and things did not look good for Kyan. At the last second, Kyan sidestepped, just out of reach of the rush of his opponent. As Matsuda went by, the diminutive Kyan kicked the man into the river. It is an amusing anecdote. And informative, as we shall see, about the strategy Kyan perfected in his karate.

Kyan Chotoku, born in 1870, only a few years after the end of feudalism in Japan, has always to me been one of the most entertaining of the great Okinawan karate masters. Perhaps it is because he was never a saint. He liked drinking and womanizing and hanging out in bars. He often encouraged his students to accompany him to brothels, saying they needed to experience the full breadth of life to become complete. He was accused of concealing money from his wife, which she earned by raising and slaughtering pigs, to use for some of these "experiences." There are many tales of Kyan's heroism and kindness, yet he was a bit of a rogue as well. In his book on karate, Katsumi Murakami devoted a chapter to Kyan called "Absorbing Both Virtue and Vice." I also find Kyan of interest because he is one of the few karateka of that era who left detailed explanations about his training. In formal interviews and in lectures to his students he gave us many hints about his methods of practice. Any discussion of these must begin with his extraordinary skills at *tai-sabaki,* or body movement.

Since Kyan was so small and slight, he preferred never to go straight up against an opponent. Instead, he would draw in an attack, then dodge or dull its edge through a shift away, then counter instantly. His encounter with Matsuda is a good example of the way Kyan liked to fight. Kyan's tai-sabaki requires eyeblink-quick movement along with the ability to move freely in any direction. Watch a karate match today and you will see movement is almost entirely forward and back. One person attacks, the other retreats, back and forth. I once spent an afternoon watching a karate competition, looking for nothing other than to see how much space the contestants used. I was surprised to see they kept almost entirely to a narrow line, rather like the *piste* strip used in fencing matches. Most bouts could have been comfortably waged in about twelve feet of an office hallway. This is fine for sport. It is limiting, however, in terms of karate being used as a fighting art. You will also likely see the participants in a karate *shiai* standing either somewhat low if they are so-called traditionalists, or in much higher stances with their legs nearly straight if they are involved in the more sport-oriented versions of karate. Neither is useful for the sort of instantaneous, multidirectional movement called for in a real confrontation. Indeed, as one of Kyan's karate contemporaries, Itosu Yasutsune wrote, "It is necessary to maintain an upright position in karate training . . . keeping a 'supple power' in the legs." The best way to train for this, according to Kyan, was to perfect the "cat-leg stance," or *neko-ashi-dachi.*

Curiously, outside of some kata, one rarely sees this stance in karate practice today—although it is worthwhile to note that in those systems that stress a lot of contact sparring such as Kyokushinkai and its derivatives, the cat-leg stance was once quite common. Goju-ryu exponents have brought the cat-leg stance to a high degree of polish and use it comfortably and to good effect when sparring. Variations abound. The most elemental form calls for the rear leg to be bent slightly, buttock in a perpendicular line with the rear heel, the front leg bent deeply enough so that only the ball of the foot rests on the floor, and the torso twisted about 45 degrees to the side.

To practice the kind of cat-leg body movement used by Kyan, it is useful to have a space on the floor where you can lay out a pattern with tape. Make a cross with the tape about three feet in both directions, then lay an X over the cross so you have, in effect, laid out stripes going in the four cardinal directions and in the four intermediary directions between them. (If anyone asks, tell them theatrically it is a "Secret Compass of Death.") Stand at the intersection, where all the lines cross, in a left-leg-leading neko-ashi stance. At the beginning, try simply to move forward and back, keeping your left leg in front, gliding as quickly and *smoothly* as you can. To move forward, you need to try to grip the floor with your left toes. Initiate movement by tensing the muscles in your inside thighs, almost "pulling" yourself forward. In other words, do not push off from the back foot. When you finish the movement, the right foot should land where the left foot was. If you have never done this, you will be lucky to gain a foot or so in the length of your stride. Much farther than that and you will lose the tenseness in your inside thighs that makes the movement quick and compresses the time that you are off-balance to a minimum. You will find, when first trying this, that you will just be stepping, with a big space or lag in your timing, a moment where you are off balance. You need to develop those inner thigh muscles to be able not just to step, but to *spring*. To do that, relax in the stance, then consciously squeeze your thighs as you move, then relax them when the step is complete. Do not think of the step as a movement where one foot leads, lands, then the other follows. Instead, think of a giant rubber band around your upper legs. When you push forward with the front leg, the back leg snaps forward immediately after.

Once you have gotten some feeling for this movement, you can make it in reverse as well. Going back, you will need again to spring off the front foot. But be careful. There should be no hip movement *up* when you make this spring back. Have someone watch you. They can point it out if your hips rise as you move backward. This rise indicates wasted time and motion. You don't want to go up, but rather back. Any energy spent moving your body up is not put into the motion to the rear: it is wasted. Eliminate that waste. Of course, this is a common problem in all karate movement: beginners do not have the musculature developed in their thighs and hips that allows for smooth lateral movement uncompromised by unnecessary vertical movement.

Don't worry about your hands or arms at this point. Do not think of your cat-leg stance as a "stance" in the sense of a fixed position of the body. (Please read chapter 26 on stance for more on the idea of the stance not as a fixed position but as a transitional phase between movements.) Let your arms hang naturally to your sides. Make an effort to relax your shoulders and release

any tension in them. You want, in fact, to isolate the tension in
your body entirely in your upper legs, and you want that tension
only at the moment you begin to move. Nothing should be slack
in your muscles, but there should be no rigidity, either. Relax,
squeeze the muscles to move, then immediately relax again.

When you can move forward and back, you should begin
working on tai-sabaki, or body movement, to the sides. Moving
to either side or in diagonal directions away from an attack (or
toward it, for that matter) are obviously the most effective sorts of
tai-sabaki in karate. They are also much, much more difficult than
basic shifts directly back and forth. Keep this in mind: When you
are moving to dodge or evade, two matters are critical. The first
is that you need to get your body's centerline off the trajectory of
the attack. The second is that you need to avoid that attack by as
little as possible. There is no need to jump three feet to the side
against a punch. If you do, you waste energy and time, and worse,
you place yourself too far away to make an immediate counterattack. It is fine to practice moving as far as possible just to get
your body accustomed to the skills required. Once you can do
that, though, you need to begin to refine the process, moving just
enough to avoid the attack, staying close enough to make your
counterattack. This is where a partner will come in handy in your
practice in our "Compass of Death." (That's a great, dramatic-
sounding title, isn't it? Maybe I could get a patent on it.) Anyway,
have him punch or kick along the line, then you move enough so
he just misses you, staying in the cat-leg stance.

Moving to the left, assuming you are still in a left-leg-leading
stance, requires you to move the lead leg first. To the right, it is
your rear leg. This is the most effective and economical way to
move laterally. Experiment with it if you don't believe me.

You should be able to see the next stage in this kind of practice.
You can begin to move along the diagonal lines of the tape. You
can move, say, facing forward at the center, off to your right front
corner, shifting direction as you move so that you end up facing the left rear corner. Facility in this kind of tai-sabaki is enor-

mously beneficial for karateka at any stage in their education. It is something that ought to be practiced regularly and studied for its ramifications. It is a tool left to us by Kyan, a man who used it himself on more than one occasion, so we would be wise to implement it in our own karate training.

17
_____

Being Uncomfortable

A martial artist reveals recently on an Internet forum that he "hates etiquette." It is not the bowing and other conventions we normally think of as etiquette to which he objects in the dojo, he posts. No, what causes him despair is confronting the landscape he has found himself in that he must navigate in pursuing a traditional Japanese budo. And understandably, he does not like the territory. Specifically, he bemoans all the awkward mistakes, gaffes, and faux pas he inevitably makes dealing with the nuances of Japanese culture that are such an integral part of these arts. One well-meant but inadvertently wrongly worded phrase in a conversation with a teacher—an innocent gesture at an inappropriate moment—and he is in trouble. Use the wrong verb by mistake in Japanese and your polite request becomes an arrogant demand.

If there is a serious martial artist out there who cannot identify with this lament, then my guess would be they are not that serious at all about their training. All of us who have worked to learn the ways of karate-do or any of the Japanese fighting arts have been embarrassed or humiliated. I am speaking of non-Japanese here. Even native Japanese, however, entering the world of the traditional martial arts are apt to make embarrassing goofs. As the generations of young Japanese grow up further and further from the feudal and immediately postfeudal Japan in which the budo were generated, they are less and less likely to be conversant in the rituals of these arts as well. I was visiting in a karate dojo in Nagano Prefecture in Japan once, watching a beginners' class. The students lined up and kneeled in *seiza*, the formal way of sitting on the knees that is a tradition in karate dojo all over the world. The sensei was in front facing the same direction, and he and the class made a sitting bow, then he pivoted to face them. And exploded.

"You are here to learn karate? How do you think you can learn something like that when you can't even sit correctly?" He was unrelenting. For nearly ten minutes he berated them. He pulled each one out of the line, had them stand, then kneel in seiza. He found half a dozen points wrong in the way they all did it. He was not incorrect in his criticisms. Their deportment while kneeling and then sitting in seiza was sloppy and slack. I watched with a sense of relief that my own posture was not currently under indictment, and ruminated that if the grandfathers of everyone in that class had lined up, sat, and bowed the same way, there would have been no lecture, no haranguing. Japanese in earlier generations were generally better educated in manners of that nature, not in the least because they spent most of their time at home sitting in seiza. (Look at the handwriting of our own grandparents' generation and compare that with the penmanship of the average modern high school kid: same thing.)

Usually blunders in the budo are entirely innocent. Most people are not deliberately slovenly or socially inept; they are just not used to the conventions of the Japanese martial arts.

For example, a karateka who has been at it a few years has decided he would like to take up the art of iaido, the formal exercises of drawing and cutting with a Japanese sword. He visits a highly ranked and respected aikido teacher who is also skilled in iaido. The teacher talks at some length about his aikido classes. The karateka listens politely, though he is really interested in the iaido instruction offered. And says so eventually, again politely. Immediately the teacher is cold, brusque, obviously insulted. Yikes.

Another example: The leader of a dojo hopes to formally present a visiting teacher with the money they are paying for that teacher to come and conduct a seminar. He goes to a Japanese department store here in the States and gets a nice envelope. He knows it is gauche to hand money over directly in such a situation. Unfortunately, he does not know that he has purchased an envelope used for giving money to the relatives of a recently deceased person, which is a funeral tradition in Japan.

A Japanese karate teacher I know once complained bitterly to me about the outrageous treatment he had suffered as a guest instructor at a big summer training camp. Among the instructors there, he was the only one who had not lived and taught extensively in the United States. He got the same information about mealtimes at the camp as did all the other sensei. Did you read it, I asked. He glanced at it, he said. But paid little attention. He expected, as would happen in Japan in such a situation, that a student would come to his room and tell him it was time for dinner. The students, not even the seniors, even gave it a thought. They had given the sensei the information and knew he could read English; he should be able to make it on his own, they assumed. He sat, waiting, wondering when he'd be called to eat, becoming angrier and angrier. At the end of the night, he had to be talked out of calling a cab, he told me, and going to the airport to fly home.

You can imagine how horrified the senior organizers of the karate camp were over this misunderstanding. I do not have to imagine. I have been in similar situations many, many times. I was once scolded for improperly holding the flask while pouring sake. My Japanese has been corrected countless times in formal situations. I got scolded once while sitting in the dojo eating tangerines after practice because I did not do it "correctly." (You tear the skin gently into four sections, in case you're interested, keeping them connected at the bottom of the fruit. After eating the tangerine sections, you discreetly spit the seeds into the bottom of the peel and fold the four sections over one another in a neat bundle.) If you have been practicing karate at all under or around Japanese instruction, you can probably think of your own goofs and social stumblings. Those whose training has been conducted in Japan will have similar tales. Indeed, it is practically impossible to read the accounts of foreign budoka in Japan who have not suffered embarrassment.

To be sure, Japan has a set of customs, etiquette, social conventions, and "unwritten rules" that are at least as complicated as any other culture, and are probably more so than most. The reason? We have to remember that Japan is, even today and certainly in its past, a remarkably homogeneous country. Japanese all share the same history, the same language, the same ways of behaving. There is little diversity. Japan was also isolated socially for much of its formative history. This has created an insular society. In Japan, one constantly hears phrases like *ware-ware nihonjin,* "We Japanese"; or *nihonjinron,* the notion of their own uniqueness that the Japanese have historically believed in. When a culture develops under the historical circumstances Japan's did, it is not surprising there are myriad details, nuances, and shared meanings within the group that are not immediately apparent to outsiders. Some of this attitude and convention reaches levels of the absurd; often one suspects or understands it to be more contrivance than anything else. Foreign rice is still almost unavailable in Japan, for example, because, as the government there explains, Japanese digestive tracts are different from the guts of other humans and cannot adequately digest non-Japanese rice. And the arcane details of some etiquette or social conventions can seem as much a form of xenophobic racism as they are a statement of Japanese uniqueness.

However, I wonder if when the Internet writer complained

that he hated etiquette, perhaps what he really meant was that
he hated to be uncomfortable. I do. I hate to be uncomfortable,
that is. I think, though, in many ways a serious study of the budo
requires one to be uncomfortable. Sometimes it is physical discomfort. The older I get, the less I enjoy sleeping on a hard dojo
floor, waking up cold and creaky, facing another day of training at
some seminar hundreds of miles from my home. Sometimes it is
an emotional discomfort. Leaving one's family to go off to Japan
or some other place for yet another period of training, being
homesick and missing loved ones; these are really an intimate
part of the budo experience. And they stink.

I have known budoka who have spent decades in Japan, and
even after all that, they are still uncomfortable sometimes in dealing with their sensei or with others in the dojo. They still make
mistakes. Sometimes a senior student or a teacher will take them
aside and explain their gaffe. Other times they get nailed publicly
and humiliatingly. Remember, I am not talking about arrogant
jerks or culturally insensitive people. And I am not talking about
beginners, but rather those who have been at their budo for a
long time and who are highly ranked in some cases. I am talking
about those who are intent on learning correctly and trying their
best. And still they endure situations that are embarrassing or
uncomfortable. The simple truth of the matter is that these feelings—the hot face of embarrassment, the sudden heavy *clunk* in
the pit of one's stomach, the bewilderment, the "no matter what
I do it's wrong" sensations—are all a part of budo. One might
avoid some of them—and only some—by having been born
and raised in Japan. But few of us have that background. We must
accept that what we are doing is outside the mainstream and certainly outside the culture in which we were raised. No one is forc-
ing us to the dojo. We have elected to take this trip all on our own.
That has some ramifications.

If we wanted never to be socially uncomfortable, never to feel
inept or awkward or out of our element, we have plenty of choices.

We can join a softball league. Or a bowling team. We can take up an activity that is a part of our culture, one where we understand the behavior and know the unwritten rules. As budoka, however, we have decided to leave a comfortable and familiar place. Bear in mind that no matter how long they have been practiced here, no matter how watered down they sometimes are, the real budo are still foreign to the West—and to the modern world in general— in a lot of ways. They have their own rules and expected conduct. They are in a special place. If we want to travel there, and spend as much time as we do in that territory, we're going to have to accept that being uncomfortable is part of the journey.

18

Finding the Model

When beginning calligraphers in Japan sit down to learn how to make the basic strokes of their art, many calligraphy schools will use *orai*. Orai are copybooks. They are compiled from copies of characters that were done by master calligraphers of the past, collected and arranged so that if, say, you want to see how Chikuso Soken wrote the character for "heart" back in 1728, you can look it up, an example of it at least, and use it as your model. You must be willing to copy it a few thousand times, of course. And your instruction must be otherwise correct. By consulting the example in the orai, though, you may assume you have a fairly good example of that character available for you to write.

In the *Jubokusho*, a fourteenth-century book on calligraphy, the importance of using these models is explained in detail. The author was Prince Son'en, a writing teacher for Emperor Go-Kogen (1352–1370). If you have visited Engaku-ji, the temple in Kamakura where the remains of the karate legend Gichin Funakoshi are interred, you will have seen when walking through the front gate an enormous piece of Go-Kogen's calligraphy mounted there. Referring to the usefulness of models in calligraphy, Son'en had this to say:

> In summation, anyone who follows a model must be in accord with it. There should be no difference between his work and the model. Those whose practice is incorrect will try to copy the form of the characters. The result will look similar. But they will fail to reproduce the vigor of the brush and their characters will lack any kind of life.

Please think about this, not in terms of calligraphy, but within the context of your karate training. However, you should know that the same advice applies in calligraphy. An orai, full of characters available for copying, is a valuable tool. In that art as well, however, you must have more than just a static model. A teacher must sit next to you, actually covering your hand with his, showing you how to move. There are places in a character where you must press down with the brush and then lift off, angles that require a deft turn of the brush that cannot be perfected or even learned without guidance. While you can and must use the copybook to learn, it is useless without a living guide to show you the Way of the brush.

In the karate dojo, our "orai" are our teachers and, sometimes, senior students. Karate and the other budo being what they are, active and full of movement, static models that are at least somewhat useful for mastering calligraphy are not nearly as valuable for us. To be accurate, they are not complete. We have books and other illustrations, and we have videos we can employ to see what "it's supposed to look like." Yet no matter how detailed these models are, at best they can provide peripheral instruction. It is surprising to me how often I am contacted by readers who explain that they do not have a teacher nearby, but they wish to pursue a study of karate or some other martial art, and what are the books I would recommend? Sorry. Books are great sources for some information, and I have shelves of them all around me. I have written several. You are, not incidentally I hope, reading one right now. So I have a vested interest in karate-do as it appears on the printed page, believe me. When I am in the dojo training, though, I am not trying to perform my side kick the way I saw it in a book. I try to do it as my teachers do it. I try to do it as the living models in front of me are doing it.

This is all well and good, and those of us fortunate enough to have such models can feel a bit smug about it. Even so, it would not do for us to feel too superior. Having a model is one step in the process. If you want to pursue a budo form such as karate-do into the upper limits of mastery, though—to really learn it deeply and well—you have to be careful, as Prince Son'en warned, about just what kind of model you are trying to copy and how you are doing it. That is to say, even if they are equal in proficiency and skill, not all models are necessarily equal in all areas.

Without hoping to appear sexist, I have noticed over the years that many more advanced female karateka do not, for all their skill, seem to be quite comfortable with their bodies. It is not that they are not skillful. I can think of half a dozen senior women karate-do practitioners I have trained with and I have learned from all of them and I deeply respect their understanding and abilities. It is not that they are not good. It is just that their techniques often seem performed as if they have been forced into a model that does not fit them. When they are moving about the dojo floor or sitting, they seem unnatural. They seem as if they are trying to make themselves conform physically to a model that just isn't right for them. Female readers may wish to take umbrage at this. It is a delicate subject and I can understand their anger at what they perceive as a slight. "I've been practicing karate for thirty years. I have earned my rank. I have trained and fought with men in the dojo. It is outrageous and unfair you would try to tell me I am not up to your lofty level of expectation simply because I am female!"

My women readers are welcome to respond with this sort of vehemence. They would, however, be missing the point. My point is to observe *not* that female karateka are not as good as their male counterparts but rather that they may have suffered from a lack of models that are most appropriate for them. Virtually none of the higher-ranking female karate-do students in the West have trained under the tutelage of other women. They have trained with men and had males as their teachers and as the majority of their training partners. Their models have been in most instances physically different from them. In some cases, where the differences are so pronounced, the model—no matter how good that model is—is so unlike the person trying to emulate him or her that the task becomes difficult. It is not easy even when the model and the student are the same in size and build and sex, of course. When they are markedly different, though, it is even more taxing.

Can a woman learn a martial art from a man? Of course. And as I said, there are women with whom I have trained and profited considerably in my own karate-do. But if you are a five-foot-eight woman who weighs 150 pounds and your karate teacher is a five-foot-three man who weighs about 110 pounds, there is going to be a disconnect between his role as a model and your ability to copy from him. The opposite is obviously more common. Most men are larger and taller than most women: if a much smaller woman is trying to learn from a larger, more muscular man, there will be some problems in communication, if for no other reason than that communication in the dojo is more often physical than in any other form. I once led an aikido seminar at a dojo where the sensei was well over six feet and weighed about 220 pounds. While he was *talking* about "blending" in meeting an attack, he was actually blocking the attacker's strike, physically interrupting it. I selected one of his students, a girl who probably moved the scales about 110 pounds and was about five feet tall. Moving slowly, I had her receive my attack and she attempted to take it as he had. I pushed right through it easily. Then I showed them both a way to receive the attack not just by talking about blending with its force but by moving so that became possible. The looks on both their faces were worth the entire seminar to me. She realized the technique could be done only if she had a partner close to her size (I am closer to her size than he is). He realized he was taking for granted his size and strength in making the technique work for him, while frustrating her when she tried to copy him.

Note again what Son'en said. We are not talking about learning technique. The technique may look similar to the model's. In the karate dojo, her Patsai kata may, on the surface, look like her teacher's, just as the characters brushed by the calligraphy student may resemble those of the model. But Son'en was talking about the vigor of the brush and the life, the vitality and the energy that appears in what is written. A human with the dimensions of that woman trying to copy the form of a man of that size will be successful to some degree if she is committed and talented at all. But mastering the essence of the art from someone so different, though, is another story entirely.

It is not only a matter of gender. Have you ever seen a slender, lithe young karateka trying to do the art like his teacher—a teacher who is a short, heavyset guy in his late fifties? I have. It is weird. I have seen young, superbly fit karateka walking like arthritic ducks because their teacher, well into his late sixties and with a lifetime of back troubles, walks that way. They are not consciously aping him; they have simply followed a model that is not appropriate. In some instances, the limitations of the teacher, in terms of size or age or build, can accidentally become institutionalized in the dojo. In the Shinto Muso-ryu, a school of the staff, the last headmaster of the ryu, Takaji Shimizu, was unusually short, even for a Japanese of that time. When he made a certain move with the jo or stick, it banged against the floor. He was just too short to keep it from touching the ground in that position. His students, including some tall Westerners, began to copy this. It became "correct" to smack the floor with your stick in some positions or movements. Fortunately, the senior students finally realized the error and corrected it. But it is easy to have these idiosyncrasies sneak into an art, all because of a particular aspect of the model.

OK, so I am advising that if you are a five-foot-two woman with short legs and narrow shoulders, you are wasting your time practicing karate-do unless you can find a teacher of the same sex and with the same dimensions, right? Wrong. Come on. If you find a good and qualified karate sensei and you really want to learn, you are nuts to pass up that opportunity, no matter what size or shape he or she is. I have made this point before: excellent budo sensei of any kind are not exactly popping up like mushrooms after a rain. They are hard to find. And during the beginning stages of your training, just follow the model that is set for you and do not worry too much about anything else. As you progress, however, you need to start thinking about the model in front of you and how or if he or she fits you. Your experience in the art will have broadened your exposure to many other fellow karateka. Some of your seniors may have body shapes more like yours. Observe how they do the techniques or the kata. Do they do them differently from your sensei? Do they seem to fit their body? The beginner will not know what I'm talking about. The more advanced practitioner, though, can recognize when a movement is natural and when it is forced and artificial.

Find models that fit you. Find those you can copy who are, in Son'en words "in accord" with you. If your sensei is radically different from you in terms of body dimensions, that is no reason you cannot learn from him or her. If you want to give your karate vitality and life, however, it eventually has to come from a model you can copy.

19

Mikiri

Stand facing your practice partner. Both of you are in a left front stance, with the left leg leading. You should be close enough so that when you swing your outstretched arms up and down, in an exaggerated motion of swinging your arms as you walk, the tips of your fingers will come up about an inch away from your partner's chin. This spacing between you and your opponent is important; we are working here on distancing, among other matters, as we shall see. Moreover, we are working on an exercise to help us understand that the difference of less than an inch can have dramatic consequences in the execution of karate-do technique. When you have swung left and right with your arms a few times and are confident in your range, bring your left arm up to the level of your partner's chin. Then draw back with your right, to chamber it as you would for the beginner's way of making a punch, fist at your right side, forearm parallel, or nearly so, to the floor. Make a right reverse punch aimed at your partner's chin. The punch should be relaxed, at a slow speed. You are not trying for speed or power at this point. What you want to do is place that punch just an inch from the target. A good way to get the right speed is to begin with a deep inhalation when you chamber the punch at your right side. Then, as your punch comes out, slowly expel all your breath so you have completely exhaled at the point where your punch has gone as far as it can go, given the length of your arm. In other words, coordinate your attack with your exhalation: both should be slow and measured.

At this point, out of breath, shift forward with both feet, sliding, and try lightly to slap his chest with the flats of both your palms, fingers pointing up. Do this as swiftly as you can once you have completed the punch. As you do, your partner slides back just as you slide forward. This stepping is called *suriashi* in Japanese, which means "sliding" or "rubbing" step. It means you and your partner are advancing and retreating without changing legs in your stance. You will have slid in toward him, left leg still leading; he slides back the same way. Having slid backward just far enough to avoid your palms hitting his chest (and not a fraction farther), he then reverses his movement, making suriashi to slide back forward quickly, at the same time aiming a right reverse punch at your midsection. You react by sliding back to avoid his attack just as he did yours, then shift forward again to make a punch back to his chin. That finishes the exercise on your side. Change to let him begin the sequence, first with the swinging, range-finding movement, then the slow punch, followed by the two-handed slap, your evasion and counterpunch, then his evasion and counter.

This exercise—it was once a standard practice in the karate dojo, though I rarely see it or any of its many variations practiced these days—is an example of *mikiri*. Literally, it can mean "cutting with the body." But *mikiri* refers to a way of dealing with an attack in a way other than blocking it. Beginners, of course, are introduced to blocking techniques quite early in their karate training. Learning to block correctly is important. All of us training in karate-do have spent hours on the dojo floor, unleashing downward blocks, inner and outer blocks, upward blocks. The movements in *uke-waza* or "receiving techniques" are usually big, broad, and exaggerated. However, once we begin sparring or other confrontations in the dojo in which the attack is not announced ahead of time and we know it is coming, we largely abandon these blocks. Nobody tells us not to do them; it just seems natural that we do not. Especially in sparring situations, blocking is almost never a good idea unless you are in a position to time it so that the block will not only stop the attack but create an opening *and* render your opponent's stability temporarily broken. That is a lot to ask of a block. Otherwise, though, a block is little more than a delaying action. Your opponent has launched an attack. You block, he attacks again; you block again. See where this is going? It is not going in a direction where you can begin to control the action. A block, by definition, means you are always responding and not initiating. You are playing catch-up. Sooner or later, if he continues to press, you are going to miss a block and his attack will get through. Blocking, at the beginner's level, is always reactive. As we advance in karate, we begin to explore ways in which it can become proactive, making it more useful in practical applications.

A lot of karate exponents in free-sparring or competition will approach the avoidance of attacks not with the stiff fundamentals taught in the dojo to beginners but with moves that either ignore or attempt to slap away incoming attacks. That is not infrequently sufficient: the way a lot of karateka attack—with poor focus and whippy, jabbing shots meant more to gain an official's attention than to inflict serious damage—avoiding or slapping them away is more than enough. When a good, high-level karate practitioner is coming at you with a strike that would, if it connected in real life, stagger you and set you up for a finishing blow—or one that would put you out of action all by itself—you need to have a better system in place, however. Mikiri is one aspect of such a system.

Mikiri requires exquisite timing and a keen sense of distancing. Have you ever seen those cartoons in which the cat will learn exactly how long the chain is that holds the big, lunging dog to its doghouse? The cat can saunter by casually, just an inch outside the periphery of the dog's maximum chain length. No matter how hard the dog lunges, how furiously it attacks, it is brought up short by the chain. All enjoyable for the cat—until the dog gets a new longer chain or it becomes so strong that it breaks its chain in mid-lunge. Mikiri is, in many ways, learning about the length of chain an opponent has. Specifically, it is concerned with being able to judge, almost by intuition, just how much reach an opponent has. This is a dauntingly difficult skill to acquire. It must be refined to the level of instinct. You cannot be thinking, "If he comes with a punch he's got about four and a half feet given the length of his legs and torso." No, you must be able to have a feel for what kind of distance an opponent has, without consciously measuring it.

There are few skills that can actually be learned and polished by the give-and-take dancing that often characterizes free sparring. Practitioners bounce and bob, shifting to and fro like the tide coming and receding. The supposed intent is to find a rhythm, then break it to your advantage. In reality, this back and forth is usually an example of what behavioral scientists call "displacement." We want to attack but simultaneously fear committing to such an action as well. So we shuffle about, making displays and threats until we can generate enough will to engage or enough fear to break off. So dancing around has limited usefulness in learning serious karate-do. Polishing mikiri, however, is one of those skills. Spending a lot of time sparring with an opponent, moving back and forth, can begin to give you some sense of mikiri. Perfecting mikiri, though, must also include static practice of the sort I have described above.

Try the exercise I have outlined. Get a feel for it. Then begin to explore some of the not-so-obvious aspects it affords. First, by punching slowly as I have described, then giving that two-handed slap-push at the end of the length of your punch, you will gain valuable insights about your own limitations in distancing. This is further facilitated by the slow exhalation that will make your timing better, consciously linking your movement to your breathing. See if you can, with practice, get a little more distance with the sliding step that accompanies the slap to your opponent's shoulders. When he makes the counterattack, see if, at first, you can shift back as far as possible from his movement. You may place yourself out of range for your own counter. But you will build the muscles and reflexes necessary to make this evasion fast and solid. (If you are not used to including stretches for the Achilles tendon in your warm-up, by the way, you might want to for this exercise. It puts a lot of strain on that part of your body. And if you do not stretch it again as part of the cooldown, prepare to have some sore lower legs the next day.)

When you are on the receiving end of the first, long, slow punch, you should take advantage of this controlled attack as an opportunity to carefully observe the kiai of your training partner. Today, we use the term almost exclusively to describe the vocalization made during kata or sparring. In classical schools of martial arts in Japan, *kiai* is often used to describe one's emotional or psychological state, especially as one approaches in preparation for an attack. Look at the way your attacker has organized his body as he prepares to step in and punch at you. Is he fully committed to the attack? Or is he already thinking of the slapping push he is going to make at the end? If you watch him, you will see hints about his mental state in his eyes and in his posture. Learning to do this as he is approaching at a slow, safe speed can make it easier to pick up on such clues during sparring.

Overall, the purpose of this exchange I have described, along with other exercises connected to the development of mikiri, is to avoid an attack by shifting out of its path, simultaneously keeping yourself close enough to be in position to make a good counter. Over time you need to gradually narrow that distance. This is a critical area where beginners often make mistakes. An attack comes at them and they retreat, which is understandable. Yet they have retreated so far they have taken themselves out of position for a counter. The trick is to retreat or evade, but to stay within range so you can respond once you have avoided or nullified your opponent's attack. At first, when you receive the punch in this exercise, you will be shifting back several inches from the farthest extension of your partner's attack. Once you can do that quickly and confidently, see how close you can stay, how close you can cut it. Eventually, he should feel he's got you until the last second, when his target suddenly fades just barely out of reach. Off balance, he is set up for your counter.

Mikiri is, as I said, extraordinarily difficult to master. But it is invaluable as a real fighting skill and its practice should never be neglected by the serious karateka.

20

Hard Training in the Old Days

Have you hit the makiwara until the skin on your knuckles has broken and begun to bleed? Good! Hit it some more! Done one thousand front kicks barefoot in the snow? That's a start! Do another thousand!

If we are to believe all the stories about the severity of karate training "in the old days," we should feel ashamed that we left the dojo last night still ambulatory. If you can walk after class, you didn't put out enough effort. At least that is how it seems regular training went in the past. It is impossible to interview the generation of karate teachers and practitioners who matured during and immediately after Japan's war years and not get the impression this was an era of karate supermen. There seems to have existed, these tales suggest, a cadre of the faithful whose devotion to karate was expressed in a physical approach to the art that was way beyond what most of us today would label as fanatical. Karate practitioners of the thirties and forties in Japan are still alive; we have their firsthand accounts: predawn, two-hour training sessions scheduled for university karate clubs, followed by afternoon and then evening practices that each lasted as long. These were the days: "bunny-hopping" exercises in the dojo that went on so long the participants pitched forward in exhaustion, too tired to protect their faces, suffering broken noses and teeth when they toppled into the floor. Training so long and so strenuously, karateka had to have assistance afterward in climbing the stairs of their dormitories. So, was this the norm for karate training in the past? And is such training necessary for a true understanding of karate? The answer to both questions is: yes and no.

First, an historical perspective is essential. As we noted in chapter 2, the history of karate from the thirties up through the fifties is an interesting one. The karateka of that period in Japan are certainly not lying about the kind of training they endured. The burnishing of memory might exaggerate a bit, but too many sources and eyewitness accounts substantiate the severity of practice, especially at the universities in Japan where karate was popular as a club activity. And in some cases I know of personally, those who lived through it might, if anything, actually downplay some of the more brutal aspects of training then. Yet it is crucial for us to distinguish between "Did they train this hard?" and "Has karate always been trained and taught this way?" While the first answer is obviously yes, the second is just as plainly no.

It is revealing, for instance, that while collegiate karateka tell eyebrow-raising stories about pounding a makiwara until the skin and flesh on their knuckles broke open to reveal the bones, Gichin Funakoshi, who oversaw much of the college karate in Tokyo, was clear in his instruction on the makiwara. If the skin blistered or broke, he said, wait at least a couple of weeks before resuming. While the young guns at Takushoku University may have been collapsing after doing a thousand kicks in 1937, one of their karate ancestors, Itosu Yasutsune, whose karate practice became the basis for teaching karate in public schools in Okinawa,

wrote a letter only thirty years earlier that advised just the opposite. "Do not overexert yourself in training," Itosu wrote, "lest your
ki [inner energy] rise and cause bodily harm." In the same letter,
he warned that if you are training so hard your face becomes red,
you are training too hard. Even Choki Motobu, one of the legendary "tough guys" of karate, an inveterate brawler and enthusiastic pugilist, constantly reminded his students that injuries, no
matter how seemingly slight, should be treated immediately. Motobu's book, among the first written on karate, contains detailed
medicinal recipes, including ingredients like goat meat, snails,
and peony bark, to cure bruises and wounds. He counseled that if
karate training became too severe, the body became susceptible
to tuberculosis. Motobu was from an upper-class family on Okinawa, and well educated. It is likely he was influenced by imported Chinese medical theories that called for great caution and
care in healing even insignificant injuries and keeping the body in
harmony through a Taoist concern for moderation in all things.
How do we reconcile this advice with the extreme attitude of "no
pain"—no risking your health and future possibilities of crippling injury or joint disease—"no gain?"

Part of the answer lies in the social and political climate of
Japan during the prewar and war years. Japan adopted an expan-
sionist, militaristic attitude at that time. Popular music and litera-
ture, entertainment, and even the native religion were all directed
by the government, all devoted to presenting Japan as a righteous
machine of war and conquest, oiled with the lubricant of Shinto
and fired by financial dreams, all of which would bring the entire
world under their control. Karate, the native Okinawan fighting
art newly imported to the mainland, was pressed into the service
of the state. It was another adhesive to cement an absolute and
binding loyalty to the government and make almost inhuman
sacrifice and commitment a part of one's consciousness. If you
can convince a guy that training until he passes out from exhaustion has some intrinsic value, it is not that tough to convince him
that suffering and dying for the empire is all that different. Severe

training in all combat arts was a part of the spirit of Japan at that time and of course, such machismo and posturing had a distinct appeal for young men who were the corpus of karate practice at that time. Whether karate leaders such as Motobu and Funakoshi and others may have disagreed with all this is the subject of debate. Whatever they felt about moderation in training, they either kept it to themselves or their voices were drowned out by the jingoistic clamor.

But what about karate as it was originally practiced on Okinawa? No doubt training there was hard. The same Funakoshi tells of walking several miles to his teacher's house and then home again in the dark after practice, utterly spent. Kanryo Higaonna, one of the progenitors of the modern Okinawan Goju-ryu, was reputed to have practiced his karate with such intensity he could only hobble the next day and he sometimes passed blood in his urine from all the exertion. Remember, however, that Okinawans in the old days, just like you and me today, had to make a living. Young men Funakoshi's age may have had the time and energy to train with fury and fire. As they got older, however, the responsibilities of work and other obligations would have interceded. In a few cases, like that of Choki Motobu, whose family had the money and status to allow him to pursue the art almost full-time, some Okinawans were able to devote the bulk of their lives to karate into adulthood. That was exceptional, however. Further, men who did physical labor could not have risked the injury or the constant exhaustion that would have resulted had karate been practiced with the intensity of SEAL training, just as they cannot today. To be sure, karate was a serious undertaking for many on Okinawa. Still, it had to be a *part* of life and not the reason for living. Funakoshi's advice about taking it easy and allowing the body to heal was practical and rooted in the everyday reality of life as an adult.

Not incidentally, people can have the same notion—that in some distant time in the past there were those who had no need to work or support a family or participate in a community—

about the samurai. They picture these "superwarriors" as training all day, every day, endlessly perfecting their skills. Think about that. It sounds romantic. But who exactly was supporting these guys? Even the wealthiest feudal lord couldn't afford to house and feed even a small army and their families. (It would not have been a good idea even if it had been possible. A group of men so removed from "real" life, constantly together in their training, would have been a constant worry for their lord. How soon before they began plotting or conspiring against him?)

Let's put the prewar and war years of Japan in perspective from the standpoint of karate-do's history. We have young, testosterone-fueled men, eager to prove themselves, all in excellent physical condition, with lots of free time—since most are in school and few have family or professional obligations. Further, they are galvanized by the rhetoric and jingoism of a nation bent on empire and glorying in a romanticized view of its warrior past. Is it any wonder they trained so fanatically and devoted so many hours of their daily life to karate?

Of course, when many of these same men began to spread karate in the West, they had only their own experiences in the dojo as a model. They naturally expected their new students to train as they had. When students asked about the "old days" of the training of their teachers, they heard remarkable stories of devotion and dedication. It is not that the stories weren't true. It is just that they were passed on without any context. The students and their teachers, both well-meaning, had no way of putting karate practice into a wider and more mature perspective. This has led to a distorted view of karate as it was originally practiced and to an approach to karate that can be unrealistic. If we looked, for example, at the time and energy an Olympic skier puts into the sport, could we adequately determine from the schedule that that is the way skiing must be approached if one expects to learn it and enjoy it? We would laugh at such a notion. And the ski industry would quickly be bankrupt. If you could not go to a ski resort without the commitment and attitude of an Olympic skier, the snow on the bunny slopes would be trackless and pristine. With an art like karate, however, we do not have a cultural outlook on it that gives us a similar view. We have, in most cases, only the stories and expectations of our teachers, who in many instances represent an intensity and approach to karate that, while authentic, by no means represents karate training as a whole.

It is hardly my intent to give lazy karateka an excuse to avoid hard training. Most of us, myself included, would do well to train harder and more often. And we ought to have high expectations for ourselves. We need disciplined goals. Yet we need to understand too that karate is not meant for the superman or, more important, for those who have no other responsibilities or obligations. On the contrary, it is for those of us who are mortal, leading ordinary lives.

21

The Art and the Way

Chosin Chibana (1885–1969) is one of the legends of Okinawan karate. In many ways, he was an archetype. He was the sort of person we might imagine when we think of the karate masters of premodern Okinawa. Chibana was a simple man, without much formal education. He worked in the sugarcane fields as a laborer or manager nearly all his life. However, he was extremely intelligent, perhaps among the best karate historians of his—or any—era. Chibana was also a natural leader. After training for about thirteen years with his teacher, Itosu Yasutsune, Chibana opened a karate dojo in a neighborhood of the Okinawan city of Shuri. When the senior cadre of Okinawan karate instructors launched a group devoted to karate research, the Karate Kenkyukai, in 1918, Chibana was elected a member, despite his comparative youth. Chibana taught karate in various places in southern Okinawa until the Second World War. Following the devastation of the battle for Okinawa, many men like Chibana were interned by the U. S. Army for a time. Chibana was sent to a camp on Chinen, a peninsula on the island. He was appointed a team leader for groups harvesting sugarcane near the camp. His talents in running a dojo came in handy in managing the workers. Chibana also organized karate training when time permitted, and he led the first postwar public demonstration of karate in 1946.

Chosin Chibana believed hard training was the only real secret to success in karate. He never wrote a book, never claimed to have founded a unique school (his followers formally christened his approach to the Shorin tradition of karate as Kobayashi Shorin-ryu after his death), never strayed from the path of karate set down by his teacher, Itosu. He was an instructor for the police department of Shuri, Okinawa. Among his proudest achievements was being presented an award from Emperor Hirohito for his contributions to karate.

Chibana began his karate training after going to Itosu in 1900 to request instruction. Itosu took him on—after first refusing the young Chibana three times in a row. In his own tenure as a teacher, Chibana had a number of followers; many of the famous karate teachers of the postwar era on Okinawa trace their lineage through him. He died in 1969 in his eighties, still teaching and training right up until the final month of his life.

Chibana was in many ways a reflection of Itosu. Like Itosu, he was obsessed with technical details. When he taught, Chibana began sessions with the first, most elemental kata. He would demonstrate and watch and would make corrections on each movement of the kata, with every student. When the next training session commenced, he would take up where he had left off in the curriculum. This is in contrast to the way some karate teachers taught at that time on Okinawa, and in contrast to the way many karate teachers worldwide instruct today. Their approach is to demonstrate the movement, having the student copy it as best they can, without offering much in the way of individual correction. In this way of learning, a student might train for several years in a kata before the teacher begins to give individualized instruction. Those who speak French will recognize this as a version of *debrouille-toi:* working it out for yourself. There is something to be said for this classical way of teaching and learning. Students learn to endure and to watch carefully when they do get instruction. With the method preferred by Chibana, on the other hand, students get a lot of attention and can make rapid progress, but sometimes they do not internalize the art as quickly. Chibana's method can sometimes be like being spoon-fed. While the contrasting method takes longer to make progress, students learn more about teaching themselves. They do not have the luxury of information presented directly. They have to search it out through repetition. (For a deeper look into this other approach, see chapter 7.) Why Chibana chose the approach he did, giving individual instruction and lots of it, is one of many questions we have about this intriguing master.

Chosin Chibana also absorbed his teacher's attitudes about the real purpose of karate. For Itosu, karate was an endless and severe tempering of mind and body, one goal of which was to kill or cripple an opponent in an instant. Itosu did not live to see much of the development of karate as a sport. There is little doubt, however, he would not have approved of it. For him, as for Chibana, karate practice was worthwhile only if it was directed to the development of the right spirit and technical (i.e., combat) effectiveness. Chibana always stressed karate's potential for lethality. Later on in his life, when asked about Itosu's influence on him, Chibana made an interesting comment. He said that according to his teacher Itosu, *do* without *jutsu* is pointless.

The apparent distinction between a do and a jutsu has been discussed many times in budo circles. "Do" is, as the word best translated implies, a Way, and as a suffix it putatively indicates a more lofty, spiritual pursuit. An art carrying the suffix of *-jutsu* is an art that supposedly indicates a more practical, technical approach to a fighting discipline, one in which spiritual or aesthetic concerns are not a primary emphasis. Some readers, I hope, will also be aware that this distinction is not at all as cut-and-dried or black-and-white as one might wish to think. The idea of a sort of yin-and-yang dichotomy is convenient when trying to describe ancient and more modern Japanese combat disciplines. It is a crude taxonomy, though. And it can lead to serious oversimplification and some inaccurate conclusions. Sometimes there is the thought, I fear, that a would-be practitioner must make a choice. Either he will pursue some art that takes him to a higher spiritual plane, makes him more "centered" as a human or in touch with others and with the universe, or he must take up an art that will teach him to be a ruthlessly efficient fighting machine. Indeed, some arts and some practitioners actually try to promote this dichotomy. "Our training is a no-nonsense approach to real-life self-defense," is an advertisement the likes of which you probably have seen. Just as you have read about places where "harmony" and "peaceful resolution to conflict" are the focus of the dojo's activities. This is all nonsense. If it is a martial art or a fighting art, it must, by the nature of the words *martial* and *fighting,* address technical combat skills. If it presumes to be an art, there must also be dimensions beyond the purely physical.

The idea that there is some legitimate budo discipline out there that somehow successfully avoids any kind of violence or physical confrontation, or teaches that such a way of life is possible, is appealing to some, no doubt. It is an idea, too, that carries with it a certain moral cachet. Surely if we are pursuing a nonviolent approach to our training, we must be more humane and thoughtful and sensitive than those sweaty and pugnacious brutes over in some other training hall, beating the stuffing out of one another. Likewise, there is an undeniable appeal, among those who profess to follow them, for those arts that feature a purely physical approach. There is a sense of superiority among their ranks. "You can talk and philosophize all day long, but we know—and practice—what *works.*"

It is unfortunate that such a phony dichotomy has been established in the minds and attitudes of so many. I have visited and trained in dojo where, paired off against a partner who is supposed to be attacking me, I have simply stood still, making absolutely no effort to get out of the way of the punch or kick coming at me. It is enlightening to watch the eyes of my "attacker." In the space of his motion, his expression goes from relaxed to confused to utterly bewildered—and often times to outright fear. He is actually afraid that his attack might possibly be, well, an *attack*. Similarly, I have trained in places where the attitude is that it is always a contest, with no intent to learn or refine but simply to bash away. Once, a teacher at a dojo where I was visiting demonstrated a technique and gave the instruction to "go slow until you get a feel for it." My partner bowed, then unleashed a vicious hooking punch at my jaw, one worthy of an amateur boxer, which I later learned he had been. I would like to flatter myself and say I escaped by my talents. In truth, I believe it was luck that allowed me to shift just enough that his fist barely brushed past my face. If he had connected, he would have broken my jaw easily. He did not know me, had no idea what my skill level was. He was pumped and ready to go and instead of trying to learn the technique or polish it, he simply wanted a contest.

The reality of budo is somewhere between these two extremes. Budo are not contemplative exercises. We can talk and read and reflect and meditate. Yet if we are going to learn the lessons of a fighting art, we must fight. We must have a physical encounter, through a free exchange of techniques as practiced in some dojo, or through the aegis of kata. (And if you have not experienced kata against a live opponent you do *not* understand kata nor have you experienced it as a method for training to fight.) If you are not in some way, prearranged or through an unrehearsed exercise, exchanging techniques, practicing some form of realistic fighting, then you are not really "doing" a martial art. Being a pacifist does not have a lot of meaning if you cannot fight in the first place: not fighting is not the same as not being able to fight.

Fighting alone, on the other hand, does not constitute an art like karate-do. There must be, as we noted earlier, some facet of the activity that opens a light on landscapes aside from the purely physical. Itosu warned that a do without an element of the jutsu is pointless. A jutsu without some kind of moral, spiritual, and aesthetic dimensions is little more than organized brutality. It is, at that, poorly organized. There is no way, lacking the framework of moral, ethical, and artistic elements, to ensure the art will attract those with the intelligence and intellectual abilities to preserve it and pass it on. Therefore, just as we are trying constantly to become stronger, faster, better at the techniques of karate-do, we must be similarly energized in looking at those aspects of our budo that address issues beyond fighting as well.

The philosophical gives meaning to the physical in the karate dojo; the physical gives life and reality to the philosophical. I think this might have been what Itosu was trying to communicate to Chosin Chibana and what, in turn, Chibana and his colleagues have tried to communicate to our generation.

22

Some Side Notes on the Side Kick

If you needed to judge the skill level of a Japanese- or Okinawan-style karateka and could look at just one of his techniques in making the determination, I suggest you ask him to perform a *yoko geri kekomi*, a thrusting side kick. The kick is iconic in karate-do. It fires out at a right angle to the kicker's body, the foot curved like a scimitar, its edge presented as the weapon. A side thrust kick has a pounding, intimidating force behind it. It usually causes the karateka's uniform to snap, adding to the sense of power. Few techniques look more awkward when inexpertly performed. Unleashed by a skilled karate-do practitioner, it is impressive. Behind its appearance, it is capable of generating tremendous force. A kinesiologist might be able to determine if this is the most powerful attack in karate. I certainly do not know. But it is an attack that involves numerous body connections and coordination, and you can easily see what a karate practitioner's got in the way of these when he makes a thrusting side kick.

Specifically, watch what the karateka does, not with his kicking or supporting leg—we will get to those in a minute—but what he does with his arms. Beginners will inevitably, if they are kicking with their right leg, flail out to the opposite direction with their left arm. Like a tightrope walker, they are trying to balance themselves. More advanced practitioners, just as inevitably, will have become comfortable with the position of extending the leg out at such an extreme angle. If they are kicking with the right leg, they will have their opposite, left arm close to their side. The fist is held in so the arm cannot be grabbed by another opponent. More important, the arm on the nonkicking side of the body is kept close in so all the power is going in the same direction as the force of the kick. The right arm in a right side kick is also usually pulled in close to the body. Many kata enforce this; in some cases the kick is performed simultaneously with a pulling action. The karateka, having grabbed an opponent's wrist or arm, pulls it toward himself as his kick goes out. This stabilizes the target to some extent. Additionally, it works to take the balance of the attacker, making him more vulnerable to the kick and preventing him from making an integrated response.

Beginners making yoko geri kekomi will also incline their upper bodies far to the opposite side of the kick, leaning way over. It isn't hard to figure out why they have this tendency: they fear losing their balance. Leaning the upper body to the right when kicking to the left, and vice versa, is an attempt to stay balanced. More advanced karateka develop the suppleness to stay largely upright as they kick, even if the level of the kick is quite high. Tae kwon do and some other combat arts that include kicks often have a different approach to this, incidentally. They will incline far to the opposite side of the kick, presumably to try to generate more power. A criticism of this is that a number of small muscles are stressed when the body comes back upright and over time this can work some damage to the back. Why stay straight? Obviously, the straighter you are, the better your vision. Your perception is skewed when you lean over. While it may initially feel natural, it is not. Lift your arm up, either one, so your fist is at the level of your nipple. Now push it straight out to the side as if you were pushing someone away from you. You will notice, of course, that your upper body does not lean at all. Indeed, if you did lean, it would not feel at all natural. This gives you some idea of how counterproductive the action actually is. Think of making a side thrusting kick as exactly that same movement, done with the leg instead of the arm.

Watching comparative newcomers demonstrating the side thrusting kick will remind you of all those people who insist they cannot ice-skate because they have weak ankles. Most of us have weak ankles if we don't stretch, strengthen, and regularly manipulate them. And they will feel that way whether it be while skating or hiking over uneven terrain or doing a side kick. That is why, however, you will see beginners thrusting out so they connect the target with the flat bottom of their foot. It is like a sideways stomp: good for pushing a boat away from the dock, but not so great as a weapon. I have a wonderful old self-defense book for women from the sixties by a "Bond girl" who was also a well-known model of the day. She illustrates this flat-foot side kick perfectly, the bottom of her sole planted flat in an attacker's gut. Both her hands, incidentally, are fixed and rigid in the classic "karate chop" position. Presumably, her acting was better than her karate.

The side kick is done more correctly by "rolling" or applying torque to the ankle so the foot strikes not on the bottom of the sole but along its outer edge. (In Japanese, this is the *sokuto* or "foot sword.") It is, admittedly, an awkward movement at first and seems unnatural. It is crucial, though, to the execution of the kick. It concentrates power in a small and focused area. Think of getting hit by a broad, flat metal ruler. Better to take the hit as a slap from the broad side of the ruler than as a sword cut along its edge, right? You will sustain much more damage from the edge of the ruler than you would from its flat side. That is the intent in a yoko geri kekomi. You need to get the edge of the foot in place as a weapon. Stand with your feet wide apart, flat on the ground, as if you were doing the second movement of jumping jacks. Now lean to the left side, squatting down so the left knee is bent, the right leg stretched out—but remember to keep the right foot planted flat on the floor. How low can you go on the bent left knee without the bottom of the right foot coming off the ground? If you want to develop a good side thrust kick, you will need to have the strength and flexibility to drop all the way down on one side, buttocks touching the ground or close to it, with the other foot still flat. (Here is a training hint: try this exercise in a place where you can push the side of your right foot against a wall where it meets the floor. This will give you more support in making the stretch.)

A major concern in making the side thrust kick is in using the muscles of the foot so the ankle isn't sprained or the foot damaged in the process of kicking. Mostly this is a matter of tightening the muscles in the foot as it bends at the ankle, which means in large part gaining more strength and flexibility in the toes. Wearing shoes as often as we do, the muscles in our feet atrophy or remain flabby. When I was young, I noticed all the senior martial artists were constantly flexing their toes whenever they were barefoot, wriggling and stretching them. I thought it might be some kind of nervous habit. Over time, I began to see it was deliberate, even if they had made an unconscious habit of it. If you develop the flexibility in your toes, you can, when making a side kick, stretch the big toe up and curl the other toes down. When you do, you will feel the muscles along the side of your shin and in your foot contract, stiffening the area on the side of your foot that you want to use as a striking weapon.

Some forms of karate call for using the heel instead of the side of the foot when making a side thrust kick. It makes some sense. But if the proper mechanics of the side kick are maintained, it means you will have to twist the ankle even farther. You should feel almost as if you are trying to stretch the foot back so the big toe is reaching for your shin to make this kind of side kick. This presents the heel as a striking weapon to best effect.

To increase the flexibility necessary to make this roll, my karate sensei had me do a lot of "dojo surfing." Sit with your knees bent so deeply the bottoms of both feet touch one another. This is called a "butterfly" in a lot of stretching or exercise classes. Now, rock forward so you are in effect balancing on the sides of both feet. At first, you will need to use your hands to support yourself as you teeter. Over time, you can begin to balance without them, sort of "surfing," your whole weight taken on the sides of the feet as they contact the floor.

A side thrust kick is usually chambered differently than a *yoko keage,* or "rising side kick," which snaps and arcs out, striking the target in a rising motion. The rising kick is typically readied by drawing the kicking leg up so the bottom of the foot is flat against the opposite knee. In a thrusting kick, the bottom of the kicking foot is held parallel to the ground or slanted in slightly. Watch the knee of the kicking foot at this point. The higher it is, the greater range the kicker has. This is no place to get into the "high kicks are/aren't realistic" debate. The more flexibility the kicker has in lifting that knee, however, the wider the options in targeting.

What about the supporting leg? In many ways, it is as critical as the kicking leg in delivering a good yoko geri kekomi. A beginner's supporting leg is usually locked at the knee. (This is one reason, by the way, that were I teaching karate and had to judge at rank promotions, I would have those tested wear a T-shirt and shorts instead of a keikogi. It is so much easier to see points like this.) There is simply no way, with the supporting leg locked in this position, that power can be transmitted effectively. The reason is that the big muscles of the hips cannot be brought into play. Instead of a straight supporting leg, the karateka strives for a springiness in the knee. It is not bent so much as it is relaxed, the muscles just tensed along the outside of the calf and thigh. Think of pushing a car out of the snow. In the first instance, you lock your legs straight and try to push. In the second, you bend them slightly, bringing your hips and lower back into the action. The second one works better. Another way to get a feel for this is to stand with your right side just touching a doorway. Lean your hip against the doorway as if you were trying to push it. Your left leg will automatically bend a little, both to provide support and to allow your hip to move sideways into the motion. That degree of bend is much like what you are looking for in the supporting leg of a side kick.

The thrusting side kick is, as I said, an excellent standard by which to measure the skills of a karateka. Mastering it, learning to use it effectively and with good body mechanics, is vital to making sound progress in karate.

23

Competition as a Battlefield

Warming up [for competition] is OK. But this must be done out-side the dojo before the competition. If this is not done, then the fighter is jumping about; he is not inwardly calm and he is not concentrating on and harmonizing with his opponent.

Those are the words of advice, given several years ago, by the well-known competitor and karate teacher, Hirokazu Kanazawa. Younger readers may not know the name. That is a pity. Kanazawa's expertise as a contestant back in the fifties and sixties was a significant factor in the emergence of the competitive side of karate, initially in Japan and later throughout the rest of the world. In 1957, he won the All-Japan Championship—with a broken hand. Kanazawa, a graduate of the instructor training program of the Japan Karate Association, became a popular karate teacher, first in Hawaii and later in England. He has taught thousands of students in clinics all over the world and has been an inspiration to thousands more. It is regrettable that there are few videos of the early days of karate competition in Japan. If you were lucky enough to have seen Kanazawa in action, or even if you have watched some of the grainy old black-and-white footage that is still around, his style was unmistakable. It was deceptively simple. The attacks he used often seemed like those of a beginner's basics, front kicks and straight punches. If you looked carefully, though, you saw he was constantly manipulating angles and working in body shifts that made the linear actually circular, the target struck at an odd, unexpected angle. An opponent's defense would seem solid, impenetrable. Kanazawa's front kick would seem to be right on line going directly into the strongest part of that defense; there was no way it could penetrate. Amazingly, though, it did. In spite of this artistry, Kanazawa's approach in competition was always fearless and straightforward. Watching him, one never had the feeling of watching a sport. For Kanazawa, it always seemed like a *shinken shobu*—a "fight with real swords." So any advice he has given on competition seems to me worth considering— especially the words he had to say about warming up.

A current opinion holds sway in the world of karate-do that contests, or *shiai*, are an almost entirely separate entity from the world of karate as a martial Way. "It's a game of tag." "Karate-do isn't about winning trophies or being a 'champion.'" The sporting side of the art is perceived by many as unconnected to the realm of karate's spiritual and moral values. It is, in fact, often consid- ered tawdry, a sort of sideshow spectacle, all about flashy moves and scoring points. So-called purists—like me—are often ac- cused of disdaining competition and sneering or dismissing the shiai as not "real karate-do." While there are those who criticize shiai, to characterize everyone who has concerns about its role in the art is inaccurate. There are karateka who pursue karate for reasons beyond winning trophies who nevertheless still see some value in shiai. Many of those critical of shiai do not object to karate competition per se. Their concerns are rather to the destinations of the road that competition can lead to, places that can take one further from the realities of karate that are so important to its overall understanding. It is not that shiai is evil. Nor is it necessarily antithetical to the development of the karateka as a sincere person serious about following karate as a Way. The danger of shiai for the karateka is not in the competition. The danger is, rather, in improper perception of what shiai is and how it should be treated. I like what Kanazawa said about warming up prior to engaging in a contest for shiai because it is a good illustration of just what that danger can be. Further, his advice reminds us that shiai, far from being a perversion of karate-do, can be a valuable vehicle for understanding the deeper aspects of the art.

Some karateka who are enthusiastic about sport-oriented tournaments insist that these unrehearsed matches offer a sense of karate as a true combat form: no sterile, robotic kata; no predetermined moves against an opponent who knows what techniques you will be using and when. In a shiai, you go in there and face an opponent and spontaneously try to score on him while preventing him from doing the same against you. The shiai provides a way to get a measure of how you might do in the heat of a real fight. Karate shiai, they say, is as close to the real thing as one may safely and morally get. Their argument is not entirely indefensible. No matter how hard you train in the dojo, there is something about being on the floor of the *shiai-jo,* or the tournament, that is different. It is impossible not to have some anxiety. Even a seasoned competitor must deal with nervousness. There are possibilities against an unknown opponent for which it is impossible to prepare. Spontaneity, even within the bounds of the rules set for the contest, introduces a new dimension for the karateka. So does the prospect of performing under the gaze of spectators, including friends and families for whom we wish to acquit ourselves well. Shiai introduces a new and worthwhile dimension to our training. It does not, however, introduce a realistic combat scenario.

The argument that shiai is as close to a real and violent situation as we might find loses a lot of its validity when we see those making it are the same ones we see carefully stretching, bouncing, and otherwise warming up before their bouts. Wait a minute. How many real-life violent encounters provide an opportunity for that kind of preparation? How often does the victim of an assault have the luxury of getting himself physically ready for a fight? "Uh, just a minute there Mr. Bad Guy. Give me a chance to stretch these tight hamstrings and then I will deliver a tornado-like spinning back kick to your head." The truth is, whatever benefits it may offer, tournament karate is about the last place I would look to learn about the real-life efficacy of the art. It is, however, a powerful and important factor in learning to polish the spirit of the karateka. Here's why: Shiai, if I understand Kanazawa correctly, must be viewed as a mental and physical process similar *in some sense* to what unfolds on the battlefield. (If you think any kind of sporting contest is any reasonable facsimile of real physical confrontation with someone who wishes you ill, our discussion here is rather pointless.) Just as in a real war, the actual fighting comprises only a fraction of the time spent preparing for that fight. Samurai, soldiers, or combatants, throughout the history of warfare, have had to deal with hours and days of waiting. It is a mistake, though, to believe that waiting time is nonproductive. Professional men-at-arms have always learned to use and manipulate the intervals between fighting to their advantage. A less-skilled soldier, whether it was a Greek hoplite, a Japanese samurai, or a modern infantryman, can actually wear himself to total exhaustion just waiting. He frets. Stews. He indulges in all sort of activities, recleaning or rechecking an already clean and checked weapon. These chores may be almost compulsive, serving—consciously or unconsciously—to distract him from the threat he knows he may soon face. Worry and unnecessary busywork drain energy. The veteran knows how to sit and wait without burning any of that energy. Further, the individual going into an antagonistic situation who is distracted may also miss critical clues his opponent can present that might make the fight more advantageous for him. In an old scroll devoted to military strategy in one classical school of martial arts is the admonition to sit quietly at night and to watch the campfires of the enemy. If you saw shadows and figures crossing in the firelight, you knew they were either moving about in anxiety or trying to make some kind of nighttime maneuver.

Of course, it is possible to read too much into this. And I cannot stress strongly enough that shiai, no matter how spirited or intense, is still and always will be play. It is not war. The sense of confrontation in a contest is nothing at all like the sensation of going out to fight, intent on killing an enemy with the knowledge that he is dead set on making you dead. It is also not a reasonable theater in which to rehearse a confrontation on the street or in the workplace. The dynamics are entirely different. But the guy who goes into a competition and treats it like nothing more than sport, who comes into the area around the contest arena and starts warming up as he would at a gymnastics meet, is making at least two mistakes, if we look at his behavior through the lens of Kanazawa's advice.

First, he is giving his opponent potentially important information about himself. The karateka warming up on the sidelines is demonstrating his own strengths and weaknesses, to some extent. Are you favoring one leg when you stretch? If so, I know that is probably your weak side. Are you wincing a bit when you stretch you shoulders? Maybe one of them is injured or is in the process of recovering.

Second, the karateka warming up is focusing on his stretching or some other part of a routine to prepare himself and so he is not seeing what is going on around him. He is not observing with any kind of sufficient attention his opponents. Notice that Kanazawa said that one ought to be using that time to "harmonize with the opponent." This is an expression of the sort we see again and again in one form or another in old teaching scrolls from classical martial arts. Often we interpret this as a "let's all get along" attitude in which reconciliation and walking through the meadow holding hands is what is intended. In the budo, harmonizing with an opponent means getting into his rhythm and getting in tune with his strategy in order to defeat him or to nullify the threat he presents. Consider that the first step in beating someone is getting in sync with him to assess his strengths and weaknesses. One way to do that obviously is to observe him. You cannot do that if you are busy warming up.

The karateka who treats competition with the same soberness and intensity as real life concentrates on the people he will be dealing with. He refrains from giving anything away about himself, trying to learn at the same time what is going on around him. It is a good strategy for the karateka at a tournament. It is also a good strategy for the karateka in life.

24

Spontaneity

A great old *New Yorker* cartoon pictures a trio of scientists observing a pair of mice running through a maze. In the caption, one scientist is telling another to observe just how much faster the mice can learn to navigate the maze—right after he throws in a cat he's holding.

Karateka often long for a way to throw a cat into a dojo full of mice. What I mean is they have an interest in introducing the element of spontaneity into their regular training. This is understandable. It is also frustrating because it is so difficult to do. How do you introduce the unexpected, the unplanned—which is a constant threat in real life—into an environment that must be, for many reasons, carefully controlled? It is almost like a catch-22 within the structure of karate training. What are you supposed to do? Go to the dojo, put on your uniform, warm up—and then wait for something unexpected to happen? Plan for something unplanned?

Much of this frustration is inherent in the basic technical nature of karate-do. Compare karate to judo. In judo, two practitioners may engage in some serious, free exchanges of techniques. Each of the hundreds of judo *waza* can be applied, full force, against a competent training partner without fear of injuring that partner or worse. Assuming, of course, a competent level of ability and good health, we may throw our opponent, lock his joints at various places, even choke him, and at the end of our session we are both happy and healthy. Compare karate to kendo. Again, with the assumption we are competent, properly armored, and using the flexible bamboo *shinai* of the art and are aiming at the correct targets of kendo, we may whack away at one another. While we be may be bruised if we get too carried away, real injuries are relatively rare in that budo. Karate-do, however, is different. It is a percussive art. Strikes, with all different parts of the body—and aimed at different parts of our practice partners—are essential to it. Unlike kendo, though, there has never been any effective or satisfactory way to armor the body against karate's strikes. Dozens of methods have been tried. Most of them made karateka look like the Michelin Man. None, however, can adequately protect the vulnerable areas of the body that are the natural targets for karate. All armor or padding hinders the movement of the wearer, slowing him or causing him to use his body in an awkward way, contrary to what the art is trying to teach. That, needless to say, defeats the purpose. Any kind of protection tends to create as many, if not more, problems than it is intended to solve. Karate organizations are still experimenting with padded mittens that cover the knuckles, for example. It does not take a master warrior to see the problems this creates. Karateka using the mittens become sloppy in their control, punching in the belief the pads will protect an opponent in case of an accidental strike. They also encourage the use of punching to the exclusion of other techniques, narrowing instead of expanding the repertoire of the karateka.

The fact is that karate practitioners can never really test their techniques the way a *judoka* or *kendoka* might. They can never "see if it really works"—and this passes through the mind of every karateka, no matter how altruistic or idealistic might be his goals in training.

One solution often undertaken by ambitious karateka is to set up situations that add an element of the chaotic or unstructured. These can be imaginative. One dojo I know of considered having occasional raids on both the restrooms and dressing rooms. They wanted the teacher to secretly select senior members, assigning them to suddenly barge in and make attacks and see how well the karateka, pants around their ankles, were able to meet the threat. Liability issues were raised; the idea was never implemented. Too bad. It would have been fun, I bet. Maybe even a little dangerous. I have met more than my share of karateka who would have little sense of humor about suddenly being grabbed from behind in their undies.

As always, there are those who seek to introduce a level of spontaneity and realism in their karate by turning to free sparring. This is a reasonable temptation. An unrehearsed match allows for a wide variety of attacks and encourages spontaneous responses. At least it is supposed to. Yet one need look no further than the karate tournament scene to see that this promise is not always met. The fact is, sparring tends to reduce responses in terms of variety and spontaneity. In traditional karate shiai, it is common for 90 percent of the points scored to come from one of two techniques: from a reverse punch or a front kick. That leads to one of the criticisms, not entirely an accurate one, of karate-do as a spectator sport: it is boring and predictable. Even in the looser, more modified versions of these tournaments, scoring is almost always achieved through back-fist strikes or flippy roundhouse kicks. Contestants, under pressure to win, fall back on comfortable techniques. That is fine for scoring points or winning a tournament. But it is the opposite of the spontaneity that so many karateka are looking for. Note here that some will argue, yes, reverse punches and front kicks most often win tournament battles. They probably also win most real-life encounters where karate is put to the test. So what's the problem? The problem is that karateka, looking for spontaneity, search for it precisely because they do not wish to practice what they already know well and instinctively. They seek unrehearsed situations where that familiar and reliable punch or kick may not be sufficient or applicable.

To understand the limitations of free sparring in learning to respond spontaneously to a combat situation, consider the sort of shooting range employed at law-enforcement academies. These are the kind where you walk through a simulated street environment, taking aim at a succession of two-dimensional villains who pop up at random spots. Which would be more realistic, a range where you could just stroll along an open street and shoot at any target that moved? Or one that required you to climb over fences, skirt around parked cars and other obstacles, and in which there were occasional pop-up figures that are clearly innocent civilians? Free sparring is like the first shooting range. You always know the parameters. Little unexpected decision-making or adaptation is needed in this arena: walk along the path and, if it pops up, it is a target, so fire away. The rules of free sparring are closely monitored, from forbidden techniques to the size of the fighting area. You know what is expected, as does your opponent. While we call it "free" sparring, you know you will not have to deal with an opponent who suddenly pulls a knife from the folds of his uniform or who snatches up a chair and heaves it at you. The goal in finding spontaneity in combat is to create situations in the dojo that are more like the latter type of shooting range, with all kinds of variables.

Typical of our era, we tend to believe we are unique and that previous generations of karateka never had to deal with this problem. The truth, of course, is that this has always been a problem. The karate practitioners of old dealt with it through, ironically, the last avenue many of us want to explore: kata.

Try it. Try just this simple exercise: Try performing your kata while wearing street clothes and shoes. Try it not on the dojo floor but in your backyard or in the garage that has been cleared of cars. And when you are supposed to make, for instance, three successive stepping punches and you find that after the second you are facing the trash can or a maple tree, you must adapt. You have to change the angle or jump back to give yourself more room or make the step suddenly much shorter. Don't stop or break the rhythm of the kata. Do not adjust and "start over." Instead, try to make the kata flow as it is supposed to. Movements may have to be compressed, angles adjusted. But see that you do not lose the integrity of the movement itself. On uneven ground and wearing shoes and clothes in which you cannot move easily, you will learn a great deal about adapting balance and stance and technique.

More important, however, try your kata against live opponents, in a structured setting. Think of a typical combination of basic techniques found in many kata: a downward block, step in, and punch; then pivot and make the same motion in the opposite direction. Each time you go through these blocks and punches, have your dojomates make the appropriate attacks or moves against which the kata's motions are intended. When you have gotten that down (and it is more difficult than you imagine—doing a kata long polished against imaginary foes is a different ballgame from one done with actual opponents in position), change the rules. Now the second attacker is free to attack a little faster, jamming your block, or pausing before he attacks—and you'll find yourself, if you are just going through the motions, "blocking" thin air. By varying his timing, he forces you to adapt spontaneously. You have to fight the programmed response your body wants to make (and this exercise is valuable *only* when you know a kata so well it is thoroughly programmed) and change to meet the different circumstances.

The next step is for one of your partners to make a different kind of attack. You are expecting a low kick and it turns into a grab. Can you go into an appropriate response? Can you go to another section of another kata without thinking about it? If you mess up, can you recover in time to meet a third attacker? The more complex the kata and the attacks, the more attackers you try to defend against, and the more you vary the timing of all of it introduces some stressful situations. The variables you can plug in—number of attackers, speed, expected response complexity—all have enormous benefit for learning to deal with combat-oriented stress situations. That, believe it or not, is a major reason kata evolved as a cornerstone of karate training in the first place.

Let's be honest. There is no way to put the cat into the maze without seriously endangering the mice trying to run it. There is no way to introduce "real life" in a combat sense to the karate dojo without putting karateka in a potentially harmful situation. Military and law-enforcement training faces the same limitations and, if you think about it, they use forms of kata to do the best they can under situations similar to those I have described. You cannot set that cat free in your dojo; you can, however, through intelligent training in kata, let the dojo mice hear the threat of the cat's purr and feel the tickle of its whiskers on them.

25

What the Kata Really Mean

Beware those who profess the ability to teach you what the kata *really* mean.

Today, there are all manner of teachers, seminars, books, and videos that purport to impart to you the "real" secrets behind the movements of a karate kata. No doubt most of these are well-meaning. And some of them may be worthwhile, but not in the sense that they can actually instruct you in some definitive, "let's get to the bottom of things, here's what it's really all about" meaning that is supposedly concealed in the kata. The value of these teaching aides is rather in the sense that they can make you step back and take a fresh look at your training. "Oh, I see that scooping block could also be used to attack the nerves on the inside of a leg." Or "the turning sequence in this kata complements the one in that kata; one is working the body this way, the other that." Teaching of this sort is always worthwhile. What is a little more questionable are claims of exclusive and heretofore concealed meanings you can glean from the kata if only you will pay for the book or video or seminar. One must be careful in accepting uncritically the revelations of a teacher purporting to possess such secrets. If someone tells you that a hooking punch is actually a triggering mechanism to release a hidden "blue chi power" in your fist that will destroy an enemy by pointing it at him, well...be a little skeptical.

What we are talking about more specifically here is the alleged notion that kata have, behind their apparently obvious practical application, technical secrets that, when unlocked, will give one special insights and skills. There may be some truth to that. To be sure, there is a lot more within the kata than the average karateka might believe. It is probably not what you might think, however. Think of it this way: How about if I told you I can teach you to write like Shakespeare? In fact, I can. I can teach you how to construct a sentence grammatically. I can teach you the fundamentals of verbs, nouns, and other parts of written speech. In that sense, I can teach you to write like Shakespeare, which is to say I can teach you the written form of the English language. I have a feeling, though, that what you hoped I meant by my promise was something a little different. You were hoping I could give you the insight, the creativity, the genius of literary spirit possessed by Shakespeare. After all, you could have—you should have— learned the elements of writing back in grammar school, right? The same is basically true of karate kata. Here is what the kata *really* are: They are tools that can allow you to internalize certain movements, to develop specific neuromuscular skills that can be useful not just as a response to some particular stimulus but as a much more dynamic and wide-ranging reaction to threats in general. They provide the basics for our own spontaneous reactions in a combat environment, just as the basics of grammar give you the tools to write your own compositions. Kata do not, as is often assumed, "tell a story" of a specific combative encounter.

Instead, they provide the skills by which karateka can tell their own stories, unique and spontaneous—and appropriate—to the circumstances in which they find themselves.

If we look at karate kata as means of teaching realistic technique, we have to wonder why anything would be concealed in them in the first place. As tools, their usefulness is in their adaptability and employment. So why hide anything? The answer again may not be what you expect. A common explanation is that the Okinawans of old had to keep their deadly arts secret from the evil, occupying samurai who were, for some reason usually left unexplained, out to get the gentle, peace-loving Okinawans. The Shimazu clan of Satsuma in southern Japan took military control of Okinawa in 1609, annexing it by threat of force. Their occupation was not so much for political control, though, as it was an economic strategy. Okinawa served as a port for Japan— a mutually beneficial relationship the creation of which did not necessitate a lot of fighting on the part of the Okinawans or oppression on the part of the Japanese. History leads us to believe that most Okinawan karate found its practical conclusions measured not against the Japanese occupiers but against other Okinawans. A good deal of premodern karate on Okinawa was confined to ritualistic dueling between villages or communities where our champion has a go at the best yours has to offer. Okinawa's culture could never have been characterized as wild and lawless: bandits did not roam the countryside as they did, for example, in China, necessitating the development of weaponry to combat them. Even so, there was undoubtedly an element of self-defense in karate practice on Okinawa as well. Under these circumstances, both as a ritual form of combat and as a personal means of self-protection, karate exponents would have preferred keeping certain applications secret or concealed to maintain an advantage over attackers or challengers. In addition, a lot of Okinawan folk practices related to religion and other spiritual matters stress secrecy in rituals. So karate would have been influenced by that societal factor as well. The natural disinclination to share one's methods with those outside the village or community combined with the strategic need for keeping one's best stuff out of the hands of others, combined with a cultural propensity for secrecy in some areas of life. All these led to the hidden aspects, such as they are, of karate practice.

When Okinawan karate was introduced, first to Japan in the early twentieth century and then later to the West, there were two significant developments in regard to the "secret" meaning of the art's kata. First, Okinawan teachers in Japan did not always instruct in the not-so-obvious applications of the kata. The teachers may not have been well trained enough themselves to have even known these applications. We sometimes assume Okinawa sent its best and brightest to introduce karate to the mainland of Japan. They *were* capable men. And talented. Unquestionably, however, there were other karate experts on Okinawa who never left the island, and for good reason: their skills and reputation kept them fully supplied with students. In other instances those who introduced karate to Japan deliberately ignored the more arcane or sophisticated elements of their art. They worked hard to make karate more like native Japanese budo, stressing those elements of it that were more Japanese, ignoring those that were more Okinawan. For whatever reason, the fact is that virtually all forms of Japanese karate specifically eschewed esoteric teachings. Japanese-based forms of karate-do are deliberately *exoteric.* They were redesigned from the Okinawan originals to be more appealing to the masses, and to the Japanese masses at that. You can think of this as a "watering down"; that is a bit harsh, though. Japan at that time was still eagerly importing Western ideas about everything from fashion to the structure of education. The old, classical martial arts with their hidden techniques and secret instruction seemed archaic and anti-egalitarian. Arts that were available to all had an air of democratic openness about them that contributed to their popularity. The appeal of this wide availability should not be underestimated. Remember that Zen Buddhism, too, is a purely exoteric form of the religion. There are not any arcane or concealed secrets in its practice, unlike the esoteric *mikkyo* of Shingon Buddhism that was embraced by the samurai class.

Second, when Westerners began learning karate in Japan in large numbers, right after the Second World War, they did not have the linguistic or cultural capability to learn the finer, hidden points of kata. They were, for the most part, young, healthy, strong men who saw the pragmatic benefits of karate and who, in the limited time most of them spent in Japan, simply did not have the opportunity to pursue the art at any advanced level. If I can put you on the ground with a simple reverse punch, do I really need to spend hours and years in perfecting a sophisticated nerve strike? That is the question a twenty-four-year-old U.S. Army corporal would have asked if, in 1956, you had told him about some subtle and esoteric aspects of a kata. And so we have Japanese karate teachers and organizations who have, either through a lack of access to the "secrets" of the kata or through a deliberate dismissal of those secrets, promoted an exoteric form of the art. And we have the first generation of Western karate enthusiasts who, because of their own limitations of time and access, were usually not able to penetrate the more arcane aspects of the art, even had those aspects been available to them. Add to this the fact that the Okinawans themselves, for many reasons, did not embrace teaching these subtle aspects on a wide scale. Itosu Yasutsune, whose contributions to the art we have mentioned before, was charged with instructing Okinawan schoolchildren in the art. He created the five Pinan kata early in the twentieth century. He simplified these kata considerably in comparison to those from earlier times, making karate's basics easier to teach to an entire class. Secret teachings require, by their nature, one-on-one instruction. Secret techniques must be imparted directly from a teacher to a student.

This change in teaching methods had a profound influence on the analysis of kata necessary to understand meanings within them that might not be immediately obvious. A teacher with a handful of students takes an entirely different approach from one with a couple of dozen or more. Teaching is less personal in the latter case, more homogenized. This large-scale teaching of course has come to characterize karate-do in our own time. In the last couple of decades, *bunkai,* or "analysis of technique," within the kata has become a term most karateka will recognize. But if you look at training films or books from the fifties and sixties, you will see that in most forms of Japanese karate—and indeed even in the more popular Okinawan forms—the explanation for a kata's movements are extremely basic.

Now that many karateka are delving more deeply into "what the kata mean," we are faced with some interesting challenges. For instance, can these subtle meanings really be taught to a large group? Are those professing to teach them actually instructing in a comprehensive way, or are they simply teaching gimmicks or disparate tricks that don't really add up to a broad understanding? Much of modern karate lost or discarded some of the kata's secrets. The attempt is made now by many practitioners to revitalize the art with a recovery of these secrets. How well it works will be worth watching.

26

Stance

How much time should we spend training in karate's stances? That was the question posed to a karate sensei who was conducting a seminar. "I never spend much time at all training in stances," the sensei said by way of reply, "and never did." This came as a surprise to many of those attending the seminar. After all, there is scarcely a karate instruction book out there that does not include extensive advice on taking a front stance, back stance, one-legged stance, and so on. In the dojo, teachers hammer away correcting the smallest of flaws in posture. The front stance must have 70 percent (and not 71 percent, mind you) on the front leg, 30 percent on the rear. The front knee must be bent to the extent it does not extend out past the toes. Rear leg straight and locked? No. Straight—but not *locked*. And so it goes. How could this sensei not have gone through a similar process? Not polished and perfected his stances?

"I never spent or spend much time on training in stances," the sensei elaborated. "But I have spent and continue to spend," he added, "hours and hours getting into and out of stances." And that is the significant difference, and it is not at all an attempt to be pedantic or cute. If we have the idea of stances in karate as fixed, static postures that we take in a series, moving through the kata or in sparring or free-form situations in the dojo, then we miss entirely their nature and meaning and usefulness in karate-do. Exotic postures are one of those fixtures of karate and all Asian combat arts, at least in the imagination of the general public. Along with wild gesticulations preparatory to the fight (meant, we are to assume, to summon up the special powers of the Mystic East), the karate stance is evocative. When a character takes one— or at least what we think looks like one—on TV or in the movies, he identifies himself as a practitioner of some non-Western fighting system. Boxers and wrestlers seem to do just fine fighting without these exaggerated and contrived postures. One of the most recognizable images of karate in the last half of the twentieth century, however, is that of a dorky, obviously unathletic, and poorly coordinated kid hopping about, arms flailing, looking like a demented, one-legged scarecrow.

Forget about stances. Forget about posing. The rudiments of every stance can be learned in a single lesson. I did not say "mastered," mind you. One can, however, get the basic mechanics of karate's back stance, for instance, quite quickly, even though there will be mistakes. To concentrate too heavily on the details of the stance (particularly at the beginner's level) is to reinforce the idea that karate is a series of poses. This idea flies in the face of all the beginner knows to be true. He may never have been in a fight in his life. Nevertheless, he knows instinctively that unarmed combat is not effectively waged by striking a fearsome posture. Few bad guys are intimidated by your superb cat-leg stance. Even fewer are apt to scheme, "Hmm, I see my victim's foot is insufficiently rotated in the crane stance. I think I can take him."

Yes, if you demonstrate for me and teach me the basics of *kokutsu-dachi*, or the back stance, and I have never seen it or stood in it before, my rendition will not be perfect. It will be even less so the minute you ask me to begin moving, to step forward or

backward and maintain it, or to switch from the back stance to
the front stance. That is the point. Work with me on the transitional forms of movement and not on the frozen form itself. The
teacher should worry less about what the finished back stance
looks like and more on how the karateka looks going into and
out of that stance. Think of it this way: what stances did you perfect in learning to ice-skate? If we took a thousand photos of skat-
ers, we would be able to identify certain postures that occur again
and again in the process of skating. We don't think of skating
postures, however. These are transitional movements. If a skating coach were to teach the rudiments of skimming across the ice
by beginning with too much attention to static postures, students
would be on their butts quickly and often. The postures develop
through motion, not the other way around.

When humans gave up the rolling, knuckle-dragging gait of
primates and became exclusively bipedal, they gained a lot. They
lost much in the way of balance and stability. In some ways, many
activities involving play or work are about minimizing the dan-
gers or the loss of productivity that is the result of poor balance. A
person may learn to stand solidly, to maintain balance and body
integrity while motionless. Some static forms of supplemental
training in karate, such as squatting in a deep, wide stance while
performing breathing exercises, may focus entirely on this aspect
of stance. However, fighting is fluid. Success depends on your stability while you are moving. The value of having a good, technically correct left and right front stance is not nearly so important
as the ability to go from that left-to-right front stance and never
lose your balance or the fluidity of the motion. In other words, if
you want to focus on stance in the dojo, work not on point A or
point B, but on getting from one to the next. Go through a kata
slowly. Instead of pausing at the usual place, where the focus of
the strike or block is concentrated, stop at the "in-between" moments. Check your balance. Halfway through the strike, arrest
yourself and feel to see which leg is bearing most of your weight.
See if you are comfortable or if you feel like you might topple. It

is entirely worthwhile to have a class go through a kata like a sort of musical chairs—with someone calling a halt at random places, everyone freezing as they are—to study how their stance looks and feels at these odd moments. If you think you have the kata mastered, this simple exercise may come as a revelation.

The history of karate stances is a fascinating one. It is a subject that has not received the attention it deserves in the karate world. It is possible to identify, often within a decade, the era in which a photo of karate technique was taken, merely by examining the stance. Many karateka will know that among Gichiri Funakoshi's precepts was the advice that "high stances are for the advanced practitioner; low stances for the beginner" and will understand Funakoshi's intent. Learn the stance at its extreme, train your body to take the stance so it places maximum stress on your joints, muscles, and tendons, and you will naturally be able to accommodate a less severe version of it when actually fighting. Even if we accept Funakoshi's advice, however, the stances we commonly see in karate today are noticeably lower than those of the previous generations. Evidence for this shows up, as we noted, in vintage photographs as well as in those systems that have retained much of their original flavor: they tend to have higher stances. In some older Okinawan schools, such as some forms of the Shorin-ryu, the ideal width of the stance is determined this way: kneel on your left knee, then place your fist in front of that knee. Place your right heel on the other side of the fist. Stand, and rotate 90 degrees to the front. The distance between your feet now is the basic distance between the feet for stances in these schools.

If you do not come from one of these traditions, incidentally, practice your kata, going through it and stopping in abbreviated stances. Chances are you will find this disorienting. Karate systems that teach low, deep stances do, as their teachers maintain, develop leg and hip muscles. The other side of the coin is that the karateka comes to depend upon these low and wide stances as nice, balanced points from which to attack and defend. The lunging, driving punches and kicks that characterize many styles of karate-do look impressive. Such movement has its limitations on uneven surfaces, or muddy ground, though. There is a reason we do not see ballet performed in a vegetable garden—and it isn't just that it would distract the strawberry pickers. Ballet's dramatic poses and movements require the same flat, smooth surface as in the dojo. Learning to adapt, to generate power from a narrower, higher base that can accommodate irregular surfaces is never time wasted for the serious karateka.

To a considerable degree, the stances of much of karate-do as it is practiced today have to do with aesthetic form. They are the result of the dictates of style. Looking through old books on the art, we see a clear change in stances beginning in the mid-thirties. Stances became dramatically lower and wider, legs more deeply bent. In the first illustrations of karate technique published in the twenties, the practitioners were nearly upright. By the end of the next decade, they were of the sort we still see today in many karate dojo. This change, I think, was wrought by historical factors in Japan. Karate became incorporated in the mainstream of Japanese budo. As it did, it experienced a period of near-explosive growth. By 1930, more than a dozen Okinawan karate teachers were in Tokyo alone. The growth led to experimentation. Karate was no longer meant entirely for self-defense or for dueling matches between rural communities, the sort of situations for which it was designed. The art added an aesthetic facet. Moving in lower stances worked to strengthen the legs and hips, yes. They also *looked* nicer.

The thought of this is anathema to some karateka. Compromising function for beauty seems to fly in the face of all we strive for in karate-do. Yet modern karate-do's lower stances do not inevitably compromise the art's effectiveness. As an aesthetic element, they reflect one of the four aspects, along with inculcating moral values, physical training, and personal protection, that comprise all modern budo forms.

The beginner learns to make stances low and deep because such practice has physical benefits in terms of training the body. The more advanced practitioner explores higher stances and the application of power while using them, but returns to the lower stances in parts of the training because they make the training more pleasurable. He seeks to perfect his form, moving from stance to stance, not because he believes a perfect back stance will make him a better fighter, but because he finds the task challenging and rewarding. This may be one aspect of karate-do—and all budo—that distinguishes it from mere violent, physical brutality. It is a function of any art to express beauty in shape and form. Stances provide this. Do not mistake them for essentials of combat. But do not dismiss them as pointless either.

27

Tenkai

An older fellow I knew when I was back in my school days, Matsui Sensei, had trained in a couple of classical Japanese martial traditions, both centered on the use of the sword. He did not speak about this willingly, but only after he'd had a bit to drink, and when he did that his native Kyushu dialect kicked in heavily and I had a difficult time understanding him: he had also been in real combat. He had faced enemies directly during the Second World War. He knew what had worked, for him at least, in terms of hand-to-hand fighting. Matsui Sensei rarely had much good to say about any of the modern martial arts. Karate-do, aikido, judo: he tended to dismiss them all as noncombat exercises, more appropriate for sport than for real-life dangerous situations. He had a lot of criticism of aikido in particular. So I was surprised one day to hear him say something good about that art. Its principle of *tenkai*, he said, was wonderful. It was indispensable, he said, in learning to deal with serious, committed attacks.

To be honest, I enjoyed listening to Matsui, though I was counseled by other seniors to keep his opinions in perspective.

That is good advice, by the way. We would all do well to listen to older people more than we do. We would do well also to realize they, just like those of us who are younger, are not at the top of the mountain. Their words are neither definitive, nor final, nor come from having seen all that is to be seen. Their opinions and thoughts have been purchased through experience, however. In Matsui's case, that experience was direct and was relevant to budo, and so it meant much to me. So I listened to what he said about tenkai. I have done a lot of thinking about it, and I continue to practice and explore it.

If you do not know what tenkai is, take the kind of relaxed, mostly upright stance you use for free sparring. If you are straddling a line drawn directly below your center of gravity, a line pointing to your front and rear, probably both feet will be pointed about 45 degrees off that line. If you are right-handed, the left leg will be in front. Now, rotating on the balls of your feet, pivot 180 degrees. No step, just pivot. Rotate. If you were facing the front of the dojo originally, you are now looking at the rear, and your right leg is leading. This movement is tenkai. It seems easy. It is. When you are standing alone, balanced and relaxed, if you are even minimally coordinated, you can shift back and forth, left and right, without much trouble. Suppose now someone was thrusting a spear at your belly. The spear is narrow; you do not need to leap a foot away from the line of its trajectory. You need only to rotate, to make the tenkai movement that will take your body far enough off that line to be safe. When your life depends on it as it would in this situation, though, making that tenkai can be as if you were doing it on a tightrope, with a rocky chasm stretching out far below, and certain death waiting at the bottom. Keeping your center and your balance in making a tenkai smoothly and quickly in a combat situation is actually very challenging.

To see the possible application of tenkai a little less dramatically than the example of the spear thrust, have a training partner simulate a straightforward knife thrust to your chest. Just stand in the same sort of stance mentioned above, of the sort you would use for free sparring, with the left foot leading. When the thrust comes in, rotate on the balls of your feet. It should take you out of the line of the thrust that will just brush your midsection as it goes by. Note that your partner must be cooperative in this exercise. As soon as he thrusts and you shift by pivoting in the tenkai, he knows what you are doing. His next thrust will "lead." He will not thrust straight at your chest the next time; he will go off his trajectory to where he knows you will be going. This may be unconscious on his part. But he has to be scrupulous in stabbing where your chest is when he begins and not to where he knows you will be shifting.

At this point, you might have a good question. Why should I shift and let the thrust go by me when I can block it and send it off its intended trajectory? The average karateka, indeed, will be tempted to perform an inner block, deflecting the line of the attack and using the rotation of his hips to add power and snap. That's fine. That is a typical response to such an attack. Assume now, though, that the thrust has come when you are standing on a crowded subway car. Or walking down Bourbon Street during Mardi Gras. Space is tight. The power of that block depends, to some extent, on having a relatively wide and stable stance. If you are going to redirect the momentum of the attack, you must have a fixed point from which to do that work. Taking a stance that wide in crowded conditions is not always possible. Or consider that perhaps your arms are encumbered, when the thrust comes, both hands holding heavy bags. There are situations where the body mass has to rotate away from the line of an attack. In essence, this is the value of tenkai, when you "block" without blocking. What I mean by this is that your hip deployment will be similar to the rotation you would use for making a regular block. The hips twist just as you would in blocking. In making tenkai, though, you will continue that rotational movement of the block on around until you are facing the opposite direction from where you started.

If you are having trouble imagining this, think of someone pushing the end of a long pole at your middle. You can either push the pole aside before it makes contact, or you can rotate so the pole's tip goes past you. You do not shift your stance laterally; you merely turn, timing the rotation so the tip does not make contact.

A second, more important reason for the karateka to perfect tenkai movements becomes obvious if you consider the possibility of having to deal with more than a single assailant simultaneously or in rapid succession. I know many dojo make a big fuss over confronting multiple attackers. Think about it, though. When is the last time you were free sparring in the dojo against more than one opponent? A highlight of karate demonstrations features a protagonist surrounded by several attackers. As they rush in, the karateka deals with them, moving around and through their attacks, sometimes punching in one direction and kicking in another. It is exciting to watch. Chances are, however, the practice for these largely choreographed demonstrations is probably the only time such training takes place in most karate dojo. The truth is, most forms of karate-do are not directed toward encountering more than a single enemy. Even in those versions where such teachings exist, they are rarely if ever regularly taught or practiced, except in isolated situations such as preparing for a rank examination, when defense against more than one opponent might be part of the testing. Sporting competition has placed an inordinate emphasis on one-on-one encounters in most forms of karate. Even without competition to blame, karate has always concentrated much of its strategy on the single attacker.

Often, karateka assume that kata contain methods for fighting against multiple opponents. So if I study the kata and practice hard, I will somehow acquire the skills to take on more than a single assailant. Instead of taking this apparently magic quality of the kata for granted, the more advanced practitioner should

begin making a detailed study of where and how in the kata curriculum these methods are actually initiated. What are the angles
made by the shifts of the kata's pattern as the practitioner moves
from one opponent to the other? Examine the common kata of
most Japanese karate-do and you will see these shifts and changes
in direction are usually 90 degrees. Do any of the kata you practice include body rotations as wide as the 180-degree turn of tenkai? I can think of one. *Unsu,* or "clouds hands," practiced usually
by upper-level Shotokan- and Shito-ryu karateka, contains a tenkai done while making consecutive lower-level punches.

Even if you are convinced your karate has sufficient shifting
techniques, you should realize there is considerable benefit in
learning tenkai. Begin your study as I explained earlier, in a relaxed, mostly upright position. Using the balls of your feet, shift
around so you are facing what was your rear. Go slowly. Or don't
listen to me and do it fast. When you do, you will see that you
"over-rotate." You are top-heavy. You are moving using your
shoulders to begin the motion and that means you won't have
control when you finish. That is why you tend to totter a bit when
you make the tenkai with any speed. You have not yet connected
your hips and feet with your upper body. In one sense, the quick-
ness with which you can move your feet will determine your success in making tenkai rapidly and with balance.

When you can get around and stop while keeping your balance with your tenkai movement, have a partner stand in front
of you and slowly make a front kick to your midsection. There
shouldn't be any power to your partner's kick; you are working
on *timing* at this point. Do a tenkai to avoid the kick, letting it go
past as you turn and the kick extends past you.

When you can rotate and let the kick go past, a little bulb ought
to go off over your head. "What if I slide in a bit, as the kick starts,
then do a tenkai?" Indeed. Look where you are when the kick
fully extends if you try this. You are right at the angle where even
a slight push is going to topple your opponent who has stretched
one leg out for the kick. Your choice of counters is extensive.

Experimenting with tenkai opens all sorts of opportunities for free sparring since it changes your body's spatial relationship with your opponents in ways you've never before encountered. After you can handle the kick coming in by rotating around it, get a second partner. Have him stand behind you. Your first partner kicks, and your second partner punches toward your back. Your job is to make a tenkai around the kick and to then beat out the punch of your second partner with a thrust of your own. This is a tremendously entertaining exercise. You don't need—or want—any power to begin. Tenkai at this level is about timing and balance and correct body shifting.

OK, for homework outside the dojo, here is your assignment. Do some research. Is the tenkai rotation unique to the Japanese budo or does it occur in other combat arts? If it does, how does their tenkai compare with what you are practicing? If it isn't similar, what is it about the nature of the Japanese fighting arts that developed it? Remember, we are talking about the Japanese arts, not the Okinawan variety. What features of Japan's premodern combat could have influenced this movement? Start thinking. And keep practicing.

28

So You Want to Quit?

It just isn't what it used to be. When you first saw karate, you thought it was fascinating. Maybe, if you were still young and in school, you had to beg your parents to allow you to begin training and promise to keep up your grades if you did. Maybe, if you were a little older when you began following the path of karate, you had to rearrange your work schedule to make it to classes. Perhaps you even had to engineer some substantial changes in your life. Training in a dojo where you thought the instruction was of the quality you wanted meant uprooting yourself entirely. You moved to another city or changed your occupation in order to accommodate your karate training. To others, who saw karate-do as little more than a hobby, these sacrifices might have seemed extraordinary. Even a little crazy. Nobody gives up a good job or moves to another place in order to play on a softball team or join a bridge club. They saw your karate in a similar way. From your perspective, however, these changes and sacrifices were a small—and, in the overall scheme of things, relatively unim-portant—price to pay for following an art that utterly captivated you. Whatever you had to do, you did it and never gave it much thought. Once you entered the dojo, it became a major focus in your life. You were there for every class. If you weren't training, learning, reading about the art, or talking about it with your dojomates, then you were at least thinking about karate-do. You developed relationships in the dojo, strong friendships. There is something about shared hardships, whether in combat or among firefighters or in any other situation where tough physical effort is necessary, that inspires a particularly strong and close kinship. Karate training was less an exercise and more like an extension of your own family. And so it went, year after year, working your way through the curriculum, advancing in rank, following karate-do as it should be followed, as a Way of life.

And so now you want to quit.

It did not happen in an instant. There was no single moment, in the middle of your kata or doing repetitions of kicks, when one moment you were content and the next you were looking toward the door. The desire to quit crept up, unnoticed. Then you woke up one morning and suddenly realized it had been in the back of your mind for a long time, a subconscious tickle so unnoticeable that for some time you never even were aware of it. You probably pushed it away at first. "I'm just tired. Too much going on with work or school. Or I am merely stuck at one level in my progress in the dojo and so naturally I am a little discouraged." After a time, though, you recognized it was more than that. Karate-do, if it teaches nothing else, instills in us the sense of honesty to face things head-on. So you do. How long had it been, you ask yourself, since you really looked forward to going to the dojo? How many nights did you have to force yourself, more from habit than anything else, to head out for class? And then comes the realization: "Wait a minute, this is supposed to be good for me, supposed to make me a better person, and so how come I don't feel good about it? How come I am going to the dojo more from habit or from a desire not to disappoint my teacher and my dojomates than from any true motivation to keep this a part of my life?"

To be honest, I cannot be of much help in your understanding of exactly what it is that motivates you to want to leave your
karate practice. I have been training for a while now, in several
Japanese budo forms, and I cannot say I have ever felt the urge
to give it up. I was always worried more about some kind of injury or illness or personal situation that would limit my training.
I never got bored with martial arts, nor have I ever felt much impulse to replace them with something else in my life. I have never
felt what you are feeling. So I guess what we may conclude is that
I am a better person than you, right? Purer in my devotion. I am
morally superior, more spiritually motivated. I have loftier goals
and a more noble sense of purpose that have inoculated me from
these feelings you are having about quitting your karate.

Nonsense.

What makes me and others who follow a martial art like
karate-do for the bulk of our lives different from those who do
not is that we have found it appeals to us and it suits our needs
in one way or another. That's all. You may still be searching for
something that will do this for you in your life. You may have already found that something else and be ready to pursue it. That
is all it means. So if you wish to think of me as a noble and heroic
person, be my guest. But spare yourself the guilt.

Here is the gist of it all: If you have been serious in your
training, you have approached karate-do with the idea it is
something more than just physical exercise. Something more,
too, than just learning a method of self-defense. What is that
something more? Probably it is something you think of as
spiritual. Karate-do, you believe, has a spiritual component.
Books, your teacher's lectures, stuff you have been reading in
places like this book all reinforce that idea. Unfortunately, you
can also get the wrong impression of what that implies. If I have
taken up karate to polish the spiritual side of my nature, that is
admirable. It does not follow, however, that abandoning karate
means I have abandoned any concern for my spiritual development. I know that sounds simple. I suspect, though, that for many

people much guilt and anguish is attached to quitting karate training. Further, in their attempts to rationalize the decision to abadon karate, some students make a big mistake.

True, sometimes people quit karate training for shallow and superficial reasons. They are lazy, mostly. They have unrealistic expectations of what karate will do for them and how quickly it will do it. People quit karate, however, for good reasons as well. They need to spend more time with their education. They have jobs that require more attention. They have spouses who may need them at home. Maybe children have entered the picture in their marriage. Priorities change in our lives. Usually, this is why most of us leave the dojo. It is no more complicated than that. If we are mature about it, we may eventually be drawn back to karate when circumstances evolve that permit it. Or we may find another path in life that provides similar benefits for us. Just because you quit karate does not mean you are insincere or shallow or lacking in an impulse to have and nurture a spiritual aspect to your life.

If we are not so mature, though, we may be unable or unwilling to acknowledge this. Because we have attached this spiritual significance to karate, we may believe that ceasing our participation in it is evidence of a moral weakness on our part. "I can't just quit," we say to ourselves. "I can't stop without a good reason. I will look bad if I do." And so we resort to a basic human tendency: we look around to blame someone else.

How many times has this happened to you? You run into a former dojomate. Or in a conversation with someone, karate comes up. "Oh yeah, I used to practice," they tell you. "But there was too much politics in the dojo. Those who sucked up to the teacher got promoted." Or, "I found out some stuff about my teacher that really changed my mind about training. I can't learn from someone I can't respect." There are always such stories, it seems, from those who have quit. The implication is: "I wanted to keep training, mind you. But because something was seriously lacking in the dojo or in the personality of the teacher, I had to take the noble path and walk away from it." Sounds good. And who knows? Maybe in some instances it is true. Certainly there are a lot of creeps teaching karate. But one is always tempted to ask, "Well, did you try to find another dojo? Another martial art that may have been more suitable?" Chances are, you don't ask those questions because you know the answer. Chances are, the person wanted to quit but didn't want to admit it, so he or she came up with a manufactured story—or at least greatly exaggerated things—to make it seem more reasonable and understandable to abandon the practice.

It is probably obvious that these kinds of excuses and defenses occur all the time in all parts of life. I have never heard anyone say of his or her divorce, "It was entirely my fault. I was a poor partner and spouse." Or, "My spouse was as good as I could expect but I developed an attraction to someone else and so I left." We always want to find some reason to explain our behavior, especially one that will make us look good. What is different here, to some extent, is that the pursuit of karate as a budo, as a martial Way, is in many crucial aspects a pursuit of the truth. In our training we are seeking to reach the truth about ourselves. Karate and all the budo force us to face ourselves. Our fears, our egos, our weaknesses: all of them are tough to hide in the dojo for long. Karate-do has a way of shoving them right in our faces, no matter how hard we try to conceal them. To be less than honest in quitting karate is far worse than the quitting itself could ever be.

Look, you want to quit karate, fine. Think about it. Think about why you began in the first place and what may have changed. If you have good reasons for your decision, it is probably the right thing to do. If you have shallow and superficial reasons for quitting, that is your business. Either way, it is incorrect to think of your actions as wrong. No, the only way they become wrong is when you are dishonest with others or with yourself about your reasons. When you do that, you demonstrate that however long you spent in the dojo, you never really learned anything about karate-do at all.

29

Polishing Emptiness

The serious karateka will already know the etymology of the word *karate*. It was, from the first time it entered language in written form, most commonly rendered with the characters that mean "China" (or more accurately "Tang," referring to the dynastic empire that by extension often became synonymous in Okinawa and Japan with things Chinese) and "hand." The latter character, for "hand," remained. Under the influence of Okinawan karate teachers who immigrated to mainland Japan in the early twentieth century, the first character changed from "China" to "empty" in its written form, the same form by which it is almost always written today. I make the distinction because the pronunciation of karate did not alter: "China" is written with a different character from "empty," but both are pronounced the same in Japanese.

Gichin Funakoshi is popularly given too much credit for implementing this written change. He was not the first to do so. As early as 1905, the karate teacher Chomo Hanashiro's book, *Karate Kumite*, used the "empty" character. In 1922, when Funakoshi published his first book, *Ryukyu Kempo Tode*, he was still using the

"China" character. "Empty hand" did not replace "China hand" on a wide scale until the 1930s. A persuasive argument can be made that the overhaul was the result of growing nationalism in Japan. But that ignores an important point. When spoken, there is no difference between the homonyms, but the change made to the written form was enormous. And significant. With a few strokes of the pen or brush, karate's image acquired, concretely and obviously, philosophical connotations and dimensions that have guided its development and propagation.

Kara, written to mean "empty," is not itself specifically a philosophical term. It is used in everyday Japanese. *Kara-ibari* means "empty pride," another term for bragging or boasting that has nothing substantial to back it up. *Kara-tegata* is to write a check with insufficient funds to cover it. That well-known pestilence of our age, *karaoke*, literally "empty orchestra," means the music needs a vacancy filled—unfortunately with the voice of someone who would in most cases best leave the vacuum as it is. *Kara* is the native Japanese pronunciation of the written character. The borrowed Chinese pronunciation, also sometimes used in Japanese, is *ku*. This pronunciation also appears in normal Japanese vocabulary: *kuki* is "atmosphere;" *kusha*, an "empty car."

What gives *kara/ku* its philosophical weight is its original derivation, in Sanskrit, *sunyata*. While I am neither Buddhist nor a religious scholar, allow me to venture this definition: Sunyata is a great void of unimaginable breadth, unfathomable depth. A cosmic emptiness. According to Buddhist and Hindu thought, it is what was before "it" existed. Sunyata is not merely the absence of things; that emptiness implies despair and lack. Sunyata is an emptiness, however, in which nothing is obstructed. It is less nothingness than it is limitless promise. Imagine (and this is the last wild analogy to which I will subject you in this book) a game of soccer played in such emptiness. No boundaries. No ground below, nor even any gravity. One kick sends the ball to the distant reaches of the universe—but without any impediment to his movement, your opponent is on the ball in less than a heartbeat.

The emptiness of sunyata is not a lack—it is a state of endless potential, infinite possibilities from which anything might arise. In explaining his decision to employ *kara/ku* as the character for writing karate, Funakoshi cited a Buddhist work that has influenced many other Japanese budo, the *Hannya-shingyo*, or Heart Sutra, which contains the lines: *shiki soku ze ku, ku soku ze shiki.* "Form (*shiki*) arises from emptiness; from emptiness (*ku*) emerges form." In this we see the vast, boundless potential of emptiness—along with the inevitability of the form arising from it returning itself again into emptiness. It is an expression of a cosmic flux, always in motion, endlessly rising and falling, creation and dissolution that merge, then emerge, in a flow beyond time or human conception itself.

Its philosophical implications aside, the idea of form resolving into emptiness and emptiness emerging into form is an expression of the creative process. The ceramicist begins learning the standard essentials of the craft, in particular the shape—that is, the form—of the pots. Eventually the ceramicist transcends established form, creating unique expressions in ceramics. Yet paradoxically, the new shapes are reinterpretations of the original forms. Japanese martial artists as well found emptiness an apt metaphor for the training process. One begins formlessly, without any idea of how the task is to be accomplished. Form is taught, internalized, mastered, and the martial artist is able to go beyond it. There is a formlessness to the art of the karateka at that stage of the training where one has internalized the essence of the art. Technique bursts forth without conscious thought, without any apparent structure; always perfectly appropriate to the moment and to circumstances. He has gone beyond form, yet it was the adherence to form, an utter devotion to it, that has brought him to this stage. He is, in a sense, as formless as the beginner. His formlessness in another sense, however, is a universe away from the lack of form of the beginner. Neither is it a culmination of things. It is only one more manifestation of "form arises from emptiness; from emptiness emerges form." And so the karateka

cannot think he has arrived at some destination but rather that
he has reached one point along a continuum that will continue
to flow, surge, and ebb until he dies. Perfection is not a goal; only
a transitory part of the endless circle of the Way of karate.

Most styles of karate-do have within their curriculum a version
of the kata known as "Kusanku" or "Kanku." A variety of ways of
performing the kata exist and are practiced by various systems of
Japanese and Okinawan karate. These kata including *kara* or *ku*
in their name may differ in many ways, however virtually all have
the same distinctive beginning movement, one that does not
occur in any other kata. The karateka brings both hands together
and raises them above the head so the outstretched thumbs and
forefingers touch, creating a triangle through which he looks
upward. The hands split, separate, then slowly come down in a
big, slow, sweeping motion back to their original starting place in
front of the body, below the waist.

The movement is intriguing. Explanations for its combat-
related meaning tend toward the unconvincing and contrived.
Reaching into the topknot of hair styled with a long pin to pull it
as a weapon? Why the grandiose gesture then, instead of a more
effective, surreptitious one? Breaking a double-handed grab to
the lapels? Again, if that were the case there would be no reason
to lift the arms so high. We can conclude that the motion has at
least some measure of symbolism. Symbolic of what? Kusanku is
old; tales of its origins are contradictory at best. In one story, a
Chinese envoy introduced the kata; in others, different karate
teachers on Okinawa are given credit for its development. One of
my karate sensei many years ago suggested I think of the opening
movements of Kusanku as an expression of "form arises from
emptiness; from emptiness emerges form." The movement begins with the hands, forefingers, and thumbs just touching, the
thumbs actually in touch with the *hara*, the bottom of the abdomen, from where all coordinated power in the dynamics of Japanese art emanate. It is the hara that should initiate the movement,
not the shoulders or muscles of the arms. From that center origi-

nates motion and the beginning of the form. The arms rise until
the hands can go no higher without the gaze that follows them
being interrupted. The form is completed, full. And then abruptly
it is broken, the hands separated, quickly, decisively, and slowly
the arms move in a big circle, down, down and around until the
hands touch once more, this time along the edges of the palm,
open and empty.

The emptiness of the first position becomes form, then returns
again to emptiness. What follows, in the kata, are the first overtly
combat-oriented movements of the kata. They are, in accordance
with this continuum, emptiness becoming form again. They are
supposed to be, that is. They are not, however, either in my kata or
in the Kusanku of any karateka I have ever seen. I have watched
closely. Following my sensei's suggestion as to the symbolism
embodied in it, I have studied karateka to see what emerges after
this position where the hands are brought together once again.
In every instance, there is a preparatory move. The shoulders
twitch. The hands wind up; they are cocked before they rise. This
movement of Kusanku is never spontaneous, never form emerging directly from emptiness. Always there is a preliminary motion. I have been fortunate enough to have seen some of the best
karateka in the world demonstrate this kata. They are a thousand
miles farther along the Way than am I. But they have not elimi-
nated this unnecessary motion. They have not yet polished emptiness so completely that form emerges without undue excess
or superfluity.

I have spent many moments in the dojo studying this in my
own kata. It has become for me something like a Zen koan, one
of those questions posed to disciples by their masters, conun-
drums designed to take them beyond the realm of logic and into
a direct experience with reality. If form cannot come directly,
completely from emptiness for me, how can I ever get past that
form into the emptiness beyond the form? Maybe it is that I have
not really become completely empty, have not found the void
from which I can move without hindrance into form. Maybe

it is enough for now that I continue to try. That is in the end—or at least, from where I am now—what karate-do has become for me. A way to seek the creative freedom that, paradoxically, is attained only by a willingness to submit uncritically to the boundaries of form. A way to seek the bright light of fulfillment by polishing the emptiness.

GLOSSARY

bajutsu: The techniques and art of riding a horse in combat practiced by mounted samurai during the feudal era

batto: See *iaido*

bu: Martial or related to martial activity

budo: The martial Ways of Japan. The character *bu* connotes "martial" and *do*, as a suffix, indicates that an ethical and moral dimension is, or should be, present in addition to the technical instruction in combat.

budoka: A person who practices *budo*. The suffix *ka* is also applied to followers of other *do* forms, such as *kadoka*, a practitioner of *kado*, or flower-arranging.

bugei: A term for the martial arts. *Bu* means "martial;" *gei* means "art."

bujutsu: A term for the martial arts. See also *jutsu*.

bunkai: An analysis of technique

bushido: A very generalized term for the behavior, ethics, and philosophy of the samurai.

choshi: Rhythm; the overall pace set in a fight or encounter.

dan: A grade given in several Japanese Ways, including karate, which indicates the level of skill of the possessor. Typically, in martial arts, this grade is symbolized by a colored belt. Dan grades are usually indicated by a black belt. See also *kyu*.

dan-i: The ranking system characterized by *dan* and *kyu* grades which is used in several Japanese arts, including karate.

funponshugi: The method of teaching through copying, especially in the art of painting.

gakuga: Talents which can be taught or instilled through the learning process. See also *shitsuga.*

hara: The region of the abdomen from which physical as well as psychological power emanates, according to traditional Japanese thought.

hsing i: One of the internal systems, along with *pakua* and *tai chi,* of Chinese combat arts.

hyoshi: Timing

iaido: A martial Way devoted to unsheathing the sword, cutting, then returning the weapon to its scabbard.

iaijutsu: See *iaido*

ikken hisastu: Literally to "kill with a single strike." The *ken* of *ikken* can be written with a character to mean either a "sword" or, when the concept is referring to karate, to mean "fist."

jo: A stick used in some Japanese combat systems, that is usually more than three feet in length but less than six feet.

judoka: See *budoka*

jukendo: The art of using a rifle-mounted bayonet

jutsu: A generic term for an art or a unified collection of techniques for a specific purpose

karate-do: See *budo*

karateka: See *budoka*

keikogi: Clothes worn during martial arts practice. This word is often incorrectly abbreviated in the West as *gi.*

kekomi: A kicking action in which the foot strikes as it is driving forward

keage: A kicking action in which the foot strikes as it rises

ki: Spirit or energy

kiai: Literally a "union of the spirit." *Kiai* refers to an organized action comprised of correct body mechanics, intent, and volition. It is used commonly to describe the shout or sounds that can accompany this union.

kokutsu-dachi: A stance with the weight primarily on the rear leg with the forward leg bent and the front foot flat on the ground

koryu: A term sometimes used to designate specifically those martial arts that were developed and employed by the samurai before the end of Japan's feudal period in 1867. Literally the word means "old traditions."

kyu: A grade awarded in many traditional and modern Japanese arts. A *kyu* grade is given to lesser experienced students in these arts, in contrast to the *dan* grades given at higher levels.

kyuba michi: Literally the "Way of bow and horse." A largely archaic term for the martial and philosophical pursuits of the samurai.

ma: An "interval of space." The distance between two fighters is their *ma*. It can be used to describe all sorts of distancing, as in the space between notes of a musical performance or the timing of an action.

ma no tori-kata: The efficient use of distance between oneself and an opponent

mae-geri keage: A front kick delivered with the foot striking up in a snapping action

mae-geri kekomi: A front kick delivered with the force driving in, in a stomping action, rather than striking upward in a snap. See also *mae-geri keage.*

makiwara: A vertical post, its base buried in the ground or fixed to a floor with a pad affixed at its top, used for practicing striking techniques.

mawashi-geri: A kick that delivers the foot to the target in a large, circular, or roundhouse motion.

menkyo: A license. The word can refer to any sort of license, such as one issued for driving. In the martial arts, it typically refers to a formal certificate allowing the possessor to teach or represent the art.

mikiri: Literally "cutting with the body," *mikiri* is a way of evading an attack.

mikkyo: Esoteric practices associated with the *Shingon* sect of Buddhism

miya: In Japanese, a Shinto shrine. In Okinawa, the word is sometimes used to describe a natural area set aside for religious or ritual purposes and was once commonly associated with training sites for karate.

muay Thai: A Thai combat art that uses both legs and arms. This form has a large following in Thailand and elsewhere and employs modified rules of boxing.

mutou: A form of grappling indigenous to Okinawa

neko-ashi-dachi: A method of standing or stepping with the weight primarily on the back leg and the front leg bent so only the ball of the foot touches the ground

nihonjinron: Literally "theories" or "discussion" about the Japanese, the word is often used by Japanese to describe or rationalize their sense of uniqueness.

nuki uchi: See *iaido*

pechin: A class of pre-modern Okinawan society, roughly corresponding to the samurai caste of mainland Japan but comprising as well an aristocratic class of scholars and intellectuals.

piste: The area laid out for a match of European-style fencing

ryu: A specific lineage representing a traditional Japanese art. The word can be variously translated as "school" or "tradition." It also refers to a body of knowledge and ethos that is passed successfully from one generation to the next.

saya: A sword scabbard

seiza: A formal way of sitting on the floor in traditional Japanese culture, with the knees bent and the buttocks just touching the heels.

shiai: A martial arts contest

shiai-jo: The area or place where a martial arts contest takes place

shinai: A bundle of tightly wrapped sections of bamboo used in *kendo* to simulate, in some ways, a Japanese sword.

shinken shobu: A fight or match where real sharpened steel swords are used

shitsuga: Innate talent or abilities which cannot be taught but which are acquired naturally. See also *gakuga.*

shodan: The first level of the *dan* grades

sogo budo: "Comprehensive" martial arts; a term to designate those combat systems of Japan that incorporate more than one specialty.

sokuto: The edge of the foot, used as a weapon in kicking.

suriashi: Stepping so the feet stay in light contact with the floor. Literally "sliding step."

taiko: A Japanese style drum

tai-sabaki: Body movement

tameshiwari: A test or demonstration of breaking objects, such as boards or bricks, with striking techniques.

tegumi: A form of grappling indigenous to Okinawa

tenkai: Moving the body so it shifts 90 degrees, by rotating both feet.

uke-waza: Techniques used to block or more accurately, to "receive" an attack.

umahana-neiji: A device used to control horses by applying pressure with a stick and rope attached to their noses; it was employed also as a weapon during Japan's feudal era.

waza: Technique

wing chun kung fu: A system of Chinese combat arts

yakuza: Organized criminal gangs of Japan

yoko geri kekomi: A kick to the side using a thrusting motion

yoko keage: A kick to the side that employs a rising, snapping action.

zenpo-giri: A generic term for kicks (*geri*) delivered to the front of one's body.